Anonymus

A New Pocket Companion for Oxford

Guide through the University

Anonymus

A New Pocket Companion for Oxford
Guide through the University

ISBN/EAN: 9783741181962

Manufactured in Europe, USA, Canada, Australia, Japa

Cover: Foto ©Lupo / pixelio.de

Manufactured and distributed by brebook publishing software (www.brebook.com)

Anonymus

A New Pocket Companion for Oxford

A NEW
POCKET COMPANION
FOR
OXFORD:
OR,
Guide through the University.

CONTAINING

An accurate Description of the PUBLIC EDIFICES, the BUILDINGS in each of the COLLEGES; the GARDENS, STATUES, PICTURES, HIEROGLYPHICS, and all other CURIOSITIES in the UNIVERSITY. With an Historical Account of the Foundation of the several Colleges, and their present State.

To which are added,

Descriptions of the BUILDINGS, TAPESTRY, PAINTINGS, SCULPTURES, TEMPLES, GARDENS, &c. at BLENHEIM, DITCHLEY, HEYTHROP, NUNEHAM and STOW,

The SEATS of

His Grace the Duke of MARLBOROUGH, The Right Honourable the Earls of LITCHFIELD, SHREWSBURY, HARCOURT and TEMPLE.

A NEW EDITION, Corrected, much Enlarged, and Adorned with a PLAN of the UNIVERSITY and CITY, and Six other PLATES.

OXFORD,
Printed for D. PRINCE, and J. COOKE, near the *Clarendon* Printing-House; and Sold by J. F. and C. RIVINGTON, in *London*. M DCC LXXXIV.

See! *Oxford* lifts her Head sublime,

Majestic in the Moss of Time;

Nor wants there *Græcia*'s better Part,

 Mid the proud Piles of ancient Art;

Nor decent Doric to dispense

New Charms 'mid old Magnificence;

And here and there soft Corinth weaves

Her dædal Coronet of Leaves;

While, as with rival Pride, her Tow'rs invade the Sky.

        WARTON's Ode.

CONTENTS.

Alban Hall	Page 86
All Saints Church	7
All Souls College	39
Arundel Marbles	10
Astronomical Observatory	24
Balliol College	57
Blenheim Castle, the Seat of his Grace the Duke of Marlborough, near Woodstock	97
Bodleian Library	8
Botanic or Physick Garden	24
Brase-Nose College	45
Chancellors, Vice-chancellors, &c. List of	92
Christ-Church, Cathedral and College	78
———— Hall	79
———— Library, and Collection of Pictures	82
Clarendon Printing-House	21
Corpus Christi College	73
Ditchley, the seat of the Right Honourable the Earl of Litchfield	109
Exeter College	63
General Description of Oxford, and it's Environs	1
Governors and Heads of Colleges and Halls, List of	89
Hertford College	46
Heythrop the Seat of the Right Honourable the Earl of Shrewsbury	115
Jesus College	65
Lincoln College	67
Lists of Chancellors, Vice-Chancellors, Heads of Colleges, Professors, &c	92
Magdalen College	26
Magdalen Hall	88
Merton College	75
	Museum

CONTENTS.

Museum Ashmoleanum	Page 19
New College	47
New-Inn-Hall	87
Nuneham, the Seat of the Earl of Harcourt	121
———— Flower-Garden	128
Oriel College	71
Parish Churches	5
Pembroke College	65
Physick Garden	24
Picture Gallery	8
Pomfret Statues	10
Printing-House	21
Publick Schools	7
Queen's College	34
Radcliffe's Infirmary	23
Radcliffe's Library	22
Schools, Publick	7
St. John's College	59
St. Mary's Church	6
St. Mary Hall	87
St. Edmund Hall	Ibid.
Stow, the Seat of the Right Honourable Earl Temple, its House and Apartments	133
———, its State Apartments	138
————Gardens	139
————Temple of British Worthies	145
Theatre, Sheldonian	15
Town and County Hall	4
Trinity College	55
University College	37
Wadham College	53
Worcester College	62

THE NEW COMPANION FOR OXFORD.

General DESCRIPTION.

OXFORD, diſtinguiſhed by its illuſtrious Univerſity, and remarkable for it's Antiquity, was called by the *Romans*, *Bellofitum*. We learn, that before their Conqueſts, the *Britains* conſecrated it to the Muſes. When the Place was firſt fortified does not appear: But the Walls now remaining were probably raiſed upon ſome former Foundation about the Time of the Conqueſt. *Robert D'Oilie* erected the Caſtle, at the Command of the Conqueror in 1071. its maſſy Ruins ſhew its Strength and Extent.

King Henry I. built a Royal Palace on *Beaumont*, near *Gloucester-Green*, the Ruins of which are ſtill viſible, where King *Richard* I. ſurnamed *Cœur de Lion*, was born. Many fabulous Accounts have been collected relating to the Origin of the UNIVERSITY OF OXFORD; but Archbiſhop *Uſher* informs us, that in

King *Henry* the Third's time, 30,000 Students resided here; and *Rishanger* (who lived in the same Reign) says, that notwithstanding the Civil Wars had so much disturbed the Peace and Quiet of this venerable Seat of Learning, there were remaining 15,000 Students. *John Balliol* (Father of *Balliol* King of *Scots*) built a College, now called by his Name, in 1263: And *Walter de Merton* Bishop of *Rochester* Incorporated by Royal Charter that which is now called *Merton* College in 1274; and these were the first endowed Colleges.

In the City and it's Environs were several Monasteries, the most remarkable of which were *St. Fridefwide's*, and *Ofeney* Abbey.

The Bishoprick, which was heretofore part of the See of *Lincoln*, was erected by King *Henry* VIII. and placed first at *Ofeney* in 1542.

The Situation is on an Eminence, rising gradually from its Extremities to the Center. It is encompassed by Meadows and Corn-fields. The Meadows, which are chiefly to the South and West, are about a Mile in extent; beyond which are Hills of a moderate Height, bounding the Prospect.

The Eastern Prospect is likewise bounded by Hills at a little Distance; the Valley growing considerably narrower towards the South: But the North is open to Corn-fields and Enclosures for many Miles together, without any Hill to intercept the free Current of Air, which purifies it from all noxious Vapours. It is washed by a Number of Streams: On the East, by the different Branches of the *Cherwell*; on the South and West, by those of the *Thames*; all which meet and join a little below the City, forming one beautiful River. The Soil is dry, being on a fine Gravel, which renders it not less healthful than pleasant.

The Town, including the Suburbs, is a Mile in Length from East to West, and almost as much in Breadth from North to South, being three Miles in Circumference;

Circumference; but it is of an irregular Figure, and several airy Spaces are comprehended within these Limits, besides the many Courts and Gardens belonging to the respective Colleges.

The City, properly so called, formerly surrounded by a Wall, with Bastions at about 150 Feet Distance from each other, is of an oblong Form, and about two Miles in Circumference. *Magdalen College*, with the Eastern as well as the Northern Suburbs, which contain the Parishes of *Holy-Well*, *Magdalen*, and St. *Giles*'s, with *Balliol*, *Trinity*, St. *John*'s and *Wadham* Colleges, are without the old Walls, of which some Part remains as a Boundary to *New College*; beginning near where *East-Gate* stood, and continuing almost to the *Clarendon* Printing-house, where there was a Portal and a Chapel; some Remains of which are still visible: The Walls make an entire Boundary to the East and South Sides of *Merton* and *Corpus Christi* Colleges. The Fortifications and Outworks, raised by the Royalists in the Time of the Civil Wars, included all the Suburbs, but they are now almost entirely demolished.

The principal Street of the City runs from East to West, the entire Length of the Town, but under different Names; the *High-Street*, beginning at *Magdalen* Bridge, includes at least two Thirds of that Length; the Remainder is from *Carfax* to the End of *Castle-Street*. The *High-Street* is perhaps without a Rival; being of a spacious Width and Length, adorned with the Fronts of three well built Colleges; St. *Mary*'s and *All-Saints* Churches; terminated at the East End with a View of *Magdalen* College Tower, and the beautiful new Bridge; which consists of six large Arches, and five smaller ones. Every Turn of it presents a new Object, and a different View; each of which would make an agreeable Picture in Perspective: Whereas, had it been strait, every Object would have been seen at one and the same Instant, but more foreshortened than at present.

The second Street is that which runs from South to North, crossing the Street already described, from whence the Centre has obtained the Name of *Quater Vois*, or the Four Ways, corruptly called *Carfax*. The Conduit was erected in the Year 1610, at the expense of Mr. *Otho Nicholson*, Master of Arts of *Christ-Church*. The Water is conveyed from *Hinksey*, two Miles from the City. Mr. *Nicholson* was an eminent Traveller, had attained a great Knowlege of the Oriental Languages, and was treasurer to King *James* the First.

The South End of this second Street is called *Fish-Street*, and the other End of it the *Corn-Market*; from whence we pass into *Magdalen* Parish, and St. *Giles*'s, which form a very spacious Street, and in some respects is preferable to either of the former, especially to such as love Retirement; it having the Pleasure and Advantage of the Country, tho' connected with the Town. One End of this Street is handsomely terminated by St. *Giles*'s Church, and adorned with the Front of St. *John*'s College.

On the East Side of *Fish-Street* (commonly called St. *Old*'s, by Corruption from St. *Aldate*'s) stands *Christ-Church* College; the magnificent Front whereof is extended to 382 Feet in Length. On the same side is the Town-Hall where the Town and County Sessions, and the Assises, are held; which was rebuilt with proper Conveniences for the separate Courts, at the Expense of Thomas Rowney, Esq; late Representative in Parliament, and High Steward of this City.

The chief Bridges are, first, *Magdalen* New Bridge, over the *Cherwell*; the Terrace of which is 526 Feet long, and consists of eleven Stone Arches. The old Bridge being much decayed, and the Entrance to the

City

City both at the East and North being found very inconvenient, an Act was obtained, 11 *Geo.* III. to make a commodious Entrance through St. *Clements* to *Magdalen Bridge*, to rebuild the Bridge, to take down the Gates, to pave and light the Streets, and to remove all Nusances. In pursuance also of the same Act of Parliament, on the North Side of the *High-Street*, between *Carfax* and *All-Saints* Churches, was erected the New General Market, 347 Feet long, and 112 wide, exceeding any Thing of the Kind as well in Size as Use, in the Kingdom. The second, on the South Side of the Town, is over the *Thames*; where there is a Gate commonly called Friar *Bacon*'s Study. This is the Entrance from *Abingdon* in *Berks*, and is itself also in that County, and consists of three Stone Arches. The Third, on the West Side, is likewise over a Branch of the *Thames*, and is called *High-Bridge*. By two Acts of Parliament of the seventh and eighth of *Geo.* III. a beautiful new Road has been made at an uncommon Expense from St. *Peters le Bailey* Church through the Castle-Yard to *Botley*, which there divides to *Fifield* on the Left, and *Witney* on the Right. This single Mile, which before was a very inconvenient narrow Causeway, is now completely finished with four New Bridges, and is become as ornamental as it is an useful Key to the West and North-West Part of the Kingdom.

There are in the City of *Oxford*, and Liberties, thirteen Parishes, *viz.* 1. St. *Mary*'s. 2. *All-Saints*. 3. St. *Martin*'s, or *Carfax*. 4. St. *Aldate*'s, or St. *Old*'s. 5. St. *Ebb*'s. 6. St. *Peter*'s *le Bayly*. 7. St. *Michael*'s. 8. St. *Mary Magdalen*'s. 9. St. *Peter* in the East. 10. *Holywell*. 11. St. *Giles*'s. 12. St. *Thomas*'s, and 13. St. *John*'s.

Of the Churches which give Names to the several Parishes already enumerated, there are but four which are remarkable, *viz.* St. *Mary's*, *All-Saints*, St. *Peter's* in the East, and St. *John's*.

St. *Mary's* stands on the North Side of the *High-Street*, and is the Church to which the University resort on *Sundays* and Holidays. It is well-proportioned, and handsomely built, in the Gothic Stile. The Porch is indeed in a more modern Taste, built at the Expense of Dr. *Morgan Owen*, Chaplain to Archbishop *Laud*, An. Dom. 1637. The Church consists of three Isles, and a large Chancel, which is paved with black and white Marble. The Vice-Chancellor sits at the West End of the middle Isle, on a kind of Throne elevated some few Steps; a little below which sit the two Proctors; on either Hand, descending, the Heads of Houses and Doctors; below these, the young Noblemen; and in the Area, on Benches, the Masters of Arts. At the West End, with a return to the North and South Isles, are Galleries for Bachelors and Under-graduates; and under the Middle one are Seats for the Ladies. Adjoining to the North Isle is *Adam de Brome's* Chapel; where the Vice-Chancellor, Heads of Houses, Proctors and Preacher assemble before Sermon, and from thence go in Procession to their respective Places. The Pulpit stands in the Center of the middle Isle. In the Arch between the Church and the Chancel, is a good Organ, originally built by Father *Smith*, and since improved by Mr. *John Byfield*. The Tower and Spire, which rises from the Ground to the perpendicular Height of 180 Feet, is a very noble and beautiful Structure, and contains a Ring of Six large Bells. The Room on the North Side of the Chancel, lately repaired in the Style of the rest of the Church, is now the Common Law School, where the *Vinerian* Professor reads his Lectures.

On the Left-side of the West Window, next to the *High-Street*, is a pretty Piece of Sculpture, representing a Woman down to the Waist: It is well designed, and properly executed; though Time or Accident hath
somewhat

somewhat impaired the Face, which has been beautiful. The Hood is of modern fashion. It is remarkable that Foreigners compliment this Curiosity with their Notice, tho' it is little observed by the Inhabitants.

All-Saints Church stands in the same Street, a little to the Westward of St. *Mary's*; and is a very beautiful Fabric of white Stone. It is adorned, both within and without, with Pilasters of the Corinthian Order, an *Attic* Story and Balluftrade elegantly finishing it without, a curious fretwork Cieling, a neat Altar-Piece, and well finished throughout. This Church is 72 Feet long, 42 wide, and 50 high, without a Pillar. The Steeple is built after the Manner of some of the new Churches in *London.* The Architect, the Rev. Dr. *Aldrich*, formerly Dean of *Christ-Church*.

St. *Peter's* in the East, near *Queen's-College*, built by St. *Grymbald*, is 840 Years old; and was the first Church of Stone in this Part of the Kingdom. It was formerly the University Church; and the University still go to it every *Sunday* in the Afternoon during *Lent.* This Parish has more to boast of, perhaps, than any one in *Europe* besides: For it contains five Colleges; *viz. University, Queens, New-College, Magdalen,* and *Hertford* Colleges; three Halls; *viz.* St. *Edmund, Magdalen,* and *Alban* Halls; two Peals of Ten Bells, and one of Six; and three Organs: Two of which belong to College Chapels, where Cathedral Service is performed twice a Day; and the other to the Parish Church.

The last Church which deserves Attention, is that of St. *John's*, which is a handsome Gothic Building. We refer our Readers to *Merton* College to which it belongs, for Particulars.

PUBLIC BUILDINGS *of the* UNIVERSITY.

The PUBLIC SCHOOLS, with one Side of the Library on the West, form within a spacious Square of 105 Feet. The principal Front of the Schools on the Outside is about 175 Feet in Length, in the Middle whereof is a great Gate, with a magnificent Tower over it, in which is Sir *Henry Saville*'s Library; and the highest Apartments of the Tower are used for Astronomical Observations, and some Experiments in Philosophy; and from thence called the Observatory. Three Sides of the upper Story of the Schools are one entire Room, called the PICTURE GALLERY. It is furnished with the Portraits of many learned and famous Men, several large Cabinets of Medals, and some Cases of Books; being intended as a Continuation of the *Bodleian* Library. Dr. *Tanner*, the late Bishop of St. *Asaph*, bequeathed his valuable Collection of Manuscripts to the University, together with a Sum of Money to erect proper Cases for them; they are here deposited, near the Entrance into the Gallery; and Mr. *Willis*'s and other Collections of Books and Coins are in a small Room adjoining.

Dr. *Edward Butler*, late President of *Magdalen* College, gave 200 *l.* to carry on the Wainscoting of the Gallery: which the late Duke of BEAUFORT, in the Year 1749 approving, ordered it to be completely finished at his Expense, as a Testimony of his Affection for the Place where his Grace received his Education. This being now done, and the Pictures cleaned and repaired by Mr. *Crawford*, they are more advantageously disposed than heretofore; and their Number greatly increased by the late Benefactions.

The UNIVERSITY LIBRARY, usually called the *Bodleian*, from Sir *Thomas Bodley*, its principal Founder, is a large, lofty Structure, in the Form of a *Roman* H, and is said to contain the greatest Number of Books of any Library in *Europe*, (except that of the *Vatican*) a Catalogue whereof is printed, in two Folio Volumes.

According to *Camden*, ' The Ground on which the
' Divinity

'Divinity School was built was purchased by the
'Univerfity in the Year 1427, and upon feveral Con-
'tributions that Structure was foon begun, but inter-
'mitted, till, by the Piety of *Humphrey* Duke of *Glo-
'cefter*, it was carried on and completed.' This is
efteemed a moft elegant Piece of Gothic Architecture,
furpaffing every thing of the Kind in the Univerfity;
being well proportioned, and finifhed in the higheft
Tafte; efpeciallly its Roof. 'The fame Duke, over
'the Divinity School, erected this Library, which he
'furnifhed with many choice Volumes he procured
'from *Italy* in the Year 1440; and in the Year 1443
'a much greater Number, befides confiderable Addi-
'tions at his Death, three Years after.'

In the Year 1597 Sir *Thomas Bodley* repaired the old
Library of *Humphrey* Duke of *Glocefter*, and in 1599
fitted it for the Reception of Books. An additional
Eaftern Gallery was begun by him in the Year 1610,
and another Gallery, projected by him, was erected
afterwards. He furnifhed the Library with the beft
Books he could procure from all Parts of the World.
In Memory of which Benefaction, the Earl of *Dorfet*
caufed the Buft of Sir *Thomas* to be erected in the
Library.

Sir *Thomas Bodley* died *Jan.* 28. 1612, having provided Salaries for the Officers, and keeping the Library in Repair. He alfo left Statutes for the Government of it, which were confirmed in Convoca-
tion; and he was declared by the Univerfity to be the
Founder.

This Original Library has been prodigioufly in-
creafed by many large and valuable Collections of
Greek and Oriental Manufcripts as well as choice and
ufeful Books; the principal Benefactors to which have
been the Earl of *Pembroke*, Archbifhop *Laud* (to whom
alone it is indebted for its ineftimable Oriental Manufcripts) Sir *Thomas Roe*, Sir *Kenelm Digby*, General
Fairfax,

Fairfax, Dr. *Marshall*, Dr. *Barlow*, Dr. *Rawlinson*, Mr. *Saint Amand*, Mr. *Godwyn*, &c. which enrichments entitle it to preservation and Improvement.

This Library, and the Picture Gallery, may be seen from Eight to Eleven in the Morning, and in the Afternoon from Two to Five. In the Winter only 'till Three in the Afternoon.

The ARUNDEL MARBLES are now placed to Advantage in a large Apartment on the North Side of the Schools.

In the Logic and Moral Philosophy School is the Collection of *Marbles, Statutes, Bustos*, &c. which were many Years at *Easton*, the Seat of the Earl of *Pomfret*, and were presented to the University by the late Countess of *Pomfret*.

A Catalogue of the POMFRET STATUES, BUSTO's, MARBLES, &c. *as they stand Number'd in their present Repository.*

1. A Statue of a Grecian Lady, 7 Feet high, wants both Arms.
2. A ditto of Archimedes, 7 Feet 2 Inches high, wants an Arm.
3. A ditto of a Roman Emperor, 7 Feet high, wants one Arm and the Nose. *Perhaps modern*.
4. A ditto of Minerva, 9 Feet high.
5. A ditto of a Roman Emperor, 7 Feet high, wants one Arm. *Perhaps modern*.
6. A ditto of Cicero in the proper habit, 6 Feet 9 Inches high.—*The Drapery very masterly. He has the Sudarium in the right, and the Scroll in the left hand. The Character of the Countenance* Settled Indignation, *in which he seems preparing to speak.*
7. A ditto of a Grecian Lady, 7 Feet high, wants Arms.

Arms.———*The Drapery falling over the right Leg is finely conducted.*

8 A Column from the Temple of Apollo at *Delphos*, with the Capital and Base; and an Apollo placed at the Top, 24 Feet 6 Inches high.
9 A Statue of Sabina, 6 Feet 9 Inches high.
10 A Venus de Medecis.
11 A square Roman Altar, 1 F. 6 Inches, by 1 F. 3.
12 Terminus of Pan, 5 F. 7 Inches high, wants an arm.
13 A Statue of Minerva, 5 Feet high, wants an Arm and the Nose.
14 A Circular Roman Altar, 2 Feet 4 Inches high.
15 A Statue of a Woman, 6 Feet high, wants Arms, and Part of the Nose.
16 A Venus cloathed.
17 A Circular Roman Altar, 2 Feet 4 Inches high.
18 A Statue of Clio sitting, 4 Feet 6 Inches high, wants one Arm and Hand.
19 A Circular Roman Altar, 2 Feet 4 Inches high.
20 A Statue of a Young Dacian, 4 Feet 3 Inches high,———*Perhaps* Paris. *It is of great Antiquity.*
21 A Roman Altar, 2 Feet 4 Inches high.
22 A Statue of Antinous, 5 Feet 6 Inches high, wants a finger of the Right Hand.
23 A Grecian Lady, 4 Feet 8 Inches high, wants an Arm.
24 A Statue of Jupiter and Leda, 3 Feet 10 Inches high, wants Arms.
25 An Antique Capital, 1 Foot 6 Inches, by 2 Feet, wants a Corner.
26 A Circular Pedestal finely ornamented with Heads and Festoons of Fruit, 3 F. by 1 F. 3 I. Diameter.
27 A Statue of Scipio Africanus, or Demosthenes, 7 Feet high.———*The Drapery in a very bold Style. It is probably of some Orator; the right hand being laid on the Breast, in a persuasive Posture.*
28 A ditto of a Woman cloathed, 3 Feet 8 Inches, wants a Head.

29 A Trunk of a Woman, 2 Feet 1 Inch high.
30 A Boy with his Finger in his Mouth, 2 Feet 5 Inches high.
31 A Statue of Jupiter sitting, 3 Feet high, wants a Hand.
32 A ditto of a Woman, 3 Feet 4 Inches high.
33 The Trunk of a Woman, 2 Feet 1 Inch high.
34 Germanicus's Tomb, 7 Feet by 1 Foot 8.
35 Two Capitals with Beasts Heads, 2 F. 3 In. high.
36 An Ægyptian Chair, 2 Feet 5 by 1 Foot 8.—*Belonging to a Priest of Isis and Osiris.*
37 A Stone carved with a Claw at the End, 2 Feet 7 by 2 Feet 6.
38 A Statue of a Roman Consul, 7 Feet high, wants one Hand and Fingers of the other.
39 A ditto of a Woman, 4 Feet high, wants the Head.
40 A ditto of Flora, 3 Feet 10 Inches.
41 A ditto of Hercules, 4 Feet high, wants Hands.
42 A ditto of Diana, 4 Feet 8 Inches high, wants arms.
43 A ditto of Hymen leaning on his Torch, 5 Feet 6 Inches high.
44 A ditto of Venus half naked, 4 Feet high.
45 A Circular Altar, 2 Feet 6 Inches high.
46 A Statue of Melpone sitting, 4 Feet high.—*Perhaps it is Agrippina, in the Character of Melpomene.*
47 A Circular Roman Altar, 2 Feet 10 Inches high.
48 A Grecian Lady, 4 Feet 8 Inches high, wants Arms.
49 A Circular Roman Altar, 2 Feet 8 Inches high.
50 Statue of Camilla, 6 Feet 5 Inches high.
51 A ditto of a Grecian Philosopher, 5 Feet high, wants the right Arm.
52 A Circular Roman Altar, 2 Feet 2 Inches high.
53 A Statue of Caius Marius, 6 Feet high.——*It has a Noble Severity.*
54 A Statue of Bacchus naked, 4 Feet 2 Inches high.—*A delicate Piece of Sculpture. The Hand is added with much Address by Guelphi, from whom are all the modern Additions.*

56 A Statue of Julia, 6 Feet 9 Inches high, wants the Arms.
57 A Roman Fathom, 6 Feet 10 Inches by 2 Feet.
58 A Sphynx, 5 Feet 8 Inches long.
59 A ditto, somewhat less.
60 A Sacrifice, 2 Feet 3 by 2 Feet.
61 A Basso Relievo of a Dacian's Sacrifice, 2 Feet by 2 Feet 4.
62 Part of a Sacrifice, 1 Foot 8 Inches by 1 Foot 2.
63 A naked Trunk of an Hermaphrodite.
64 Basso Relievo, 1 Foot 10 Inches by 1 Foot 3.
65 Basso Relievo of a Shepherd, 2 Feet by 11 Inches.
66 A Bacchanalian, 2 Feet 3 Inches by 2 Feet.
67 A Woman's Head, 1 Foot 6 Inches high, wants the Nose.
68 The Trunk of a Man, 2 Feet 2 Inches.
69 A Trunk of a Woman sitting, 2 Feet 7 Inches.
70 A Consular Trunk, 5 Feet 6 Inches high.
71 A Trunk of a Woman sitting, 2 Feet 7 Inches.
72 A Bust of a Roman, 1 Foot 6 Inches high, wants the Nose.
73 The Head of a Man, 1 Foot high, wants the Nose.
74 A Trunk of Venus naked, 1 Foot 10 Inches high.
75 An Old Man's Head.
76 A Man's Head, 10 Inches high, wants the Nose.
77 Part of a Head and Neck, 1 Foot 6 Inches high.
78 An Old Man's Head.
79 A Statue of a young Satyr, 2 Feet 6 Inches high.
80 A naked Trunk of a Man, 2 Feet 6 Inches high.
81 Beasts devouring Men.—*It is the Pedestal of a Table, Scylla and Charybdis are represented devouring Mariners; whose Attitudes are extremely fine.*
82 A Trunk of a Woman, 2 Feet 8 Inches high.
83 Part of a Man's Foot.
84 A naked Trunk of a Man, 2 Feet 6 Inches high.
85 Part of two Masks, 2 Feet 5 Inches by 1 Foot 9.
86 A Lion, 3 Feet 10 Inches long.

87 An Alabaster Urn, 2 Feet 8 Inches high.
88 A Sarcophagus, 5 Feet 2 Inches by 1 Foot 6.
89 Statue of Judith, 4 Feet 6 Inches high.
90 A ditto of Hercules choaking a Lion.—*Few Figures have greater Spirit. On the Rock adjoining seems to have been the Figure of a Woman, perhaps of a Muse singing the Atchievement to her Harp.*
91 A Sarcophagus with Boys, 4 Feet by 1 Foot 4.
92 A Sea-lion, 3 F. 6 Inches long, 2 Feet 4 Inches high.
93 Dogs and a Boar, 2 Feet long.
94 A sleeping Cupid, 2 Feet 5 Inches high.—*The Lizard may be a Device for the Name of the Sculptor, unless allegorical.*
95 A Sarcophagus, 2 Feet 3 Inches by 1 Foot.
96 A Basso Relievo Roman Repast, 2 Feet by 1 Foot 7.
97 A Trunk of a Woman, 2 Feet high.
98 Soldiers Fighting, 1 Foot 11 Inches by 2 Feet 3.
99 Soldiers Fighting, 3 Feet 11 by 1 Foot 3.
100 A Trunk of a Young Man, 1 Foot 11.
101 The Triumph of Amphytrion, 2 Feet by 2 Feet.
102 A Trunk of a Woman sitting, 1 Foot 3 Inches high.
103 The Taking of Troy, 7 Feet by 11 Inches.—— *The Figures executed with amazing Expression.*
104 Boys embracing, 2 Feet 3 Inches by 1 Foot 6.
105 The Herculean Games, 2 Feet 3 Inches by 2 Feet.
106 Boys, 2 Feet by 1 Foot.
107 A Woman and a Child sitting in a square Nich, 1 Foot 9 Inches by 1 F. 7.
108 A Roman Monument with three Busts, 3 Feet 10 Inches by 2 Feet 3.
109 Part of a Roman Monument.
110 Ditto.
111 Bust of a Roman Head.
112 Bust of a Roman Head.
113 A Roman Bust.
114 A Bust of Fauna.
115 A ditto of Faunus.

116 The Bust of a Young Man.
117 A Ditto of Diana.
118 Ditto of a Grecian.
119 Ditto of a Woman cloathed.
120 Ditto of a Philosopher.
121 Philosophy, a Bust.
122 A Bust of Niobe.
123 Ditto of one of her Sons.
124 Ditto of Venus de Medicis.
125 Ditto of a Woman cloathed.
126 A Bust cloathed, wants the Head.
127 Ditto.
128 Ditto.
129 Ditto.
130 A Bust naked, Head wanting.
131 Bust of an Old Man, half naked.
132 Ditto of a Roman.
133 Bust of Hen. VIII. *modern*.
134 Ditto *(modern)* of Rob. C. Pal. Rhen. D. Bav. 1697, Ætat. 17.
135 A Colossal Head of Apollo.

Near the Schools stands the THEATRE, in Form of a *Roman* D, only longer in Proportion from Right to Left; it hath a flat Roof, composed of short Pieces of Timber, continued to a great Breadth, without Arch-work or Pillar to support them, being sustained only by the Side-walls and their own Texture, tho' from Side-wall to Side-wall it is 80 Feet over one Way, and 70 the other; which gave Occasion to say, that the Foundation was on the Roof.

When properly filled, the Vice-Chancellor being seated in the Center of the semicircular Part, the Noblemen and Doctors on his right and left Hand, the Proctors and Curators in their Robes, the Masters of Arts, Bachelors, and Under-Graduates, in their respective Habits and Places, together with Strangers of both Sexes, it makes a most august Appearance.

On the Outside it is adorned with Sculpture; particularly the Statues of *Charles* II, the first Duke of *Ormond*, and Archbishop *Sheldon*, done by *Chair*: Within with Painting, *viz.* the Portraits, at full Length, of the Founder Archbishop *Sheldon*, the same Duke of *Ormond*, and Sir *Christopher Wren*, the Architect: Likewise a curious Cieling; of which the following is a Description.

'In Imitation of the Theatres of the ancient *Greeks*
'and *Romans*, which were too large to be covered with
'Lead or Tile, so this, by the Painting of the flat Roof
'within, is represented open; and as they stretched
'a Cordage, from Pilaster to Pilaster, upon which they
'strain'd a Covering of Cloth, to protect the People
'from the Injuries of the Weather, so here is a Cord-
'moulding gilded, that reaches cross the House, both
'in Length and Breadth, which supporteth a great
'reddish Drapery, supposed to have covered the Roof,
'but now furled up by the *Genii* round about the House,
'towards the Wall, which discovereth the open Air,
'and maketh Way for the Descent of the *Arts* and *Sciences*, that are congregated in a Circle of Clouds, to
'whose Assembly *Truth* descends, as being solicited and
'implored by them all.

'For Joy of this Festival some other *Genii* sport
'about the Clouds, with their Festoons of Flowers and
'Lawrels, and prepare their Garlands of Lawrels and
'Roses, *viz. Honour* and *Pleasure*, for the great Lovers
'and Students of those Arts: And that this Assembly
'might be perfectly happy, their great Enemies and
'Disturbers, *Envy*, *Rapine*, and *Brutality*, are by the
'*Genii* of their opposite Virtues, *viz. Prudence, Fortitude*, and *Eloquence*, driven from the Society, and
'thrown down Head-long from the Clouds: The Report of the Assembly of the one, and the Expulsion
'of the other, being proclaimed thro' the open and
'serene

'serene Air, by some other of the *Genii*, who blowing
'their antick Trumpets, divide themselves into the
'several Quarters of the World.

Thus far in General.

'More particularly, the Circle of Figures consist,
'First of *Theology*, with her Book of Seven Seals,
'imploring the Assistance of *Truth* for the unfolding
'of it.

'On her Left-hand is the *Mosaical Law* veiled,
'with the Tables of Stone, to which she points with
'her Iron Rod.

'On her Right-hand is the *Gospel*, with the Cross
'in one Hand, and a Chalice in the other.

'In the same Division, over the *Mosaical Law*, is
'*History*, holding up her Pen, as dedicating it to
'*Truth*, and an attending *Genius*, with several Frag-
'ments of Old Writing, from which she collects her
'History into her Books.

'On the other Side, near the *Gospel*, is *Divine Poesy*,
'with her Harp of *David*'s Fashion.

'In the Triangle on the Right-hand of the *Gospel*,
'is also *Logic*, in a Posture of arguing; and on the
'Left-hand of the *Mosaical Law*, is *Music*, with her
'Antic Lyre, having a Pen in her Hand, and a Pa-
'per of Music Notes on her Knee, with a *Genius* on
'her Right-hand, (a little within the Partition of
'*Theology*) playing on a Flute, being the Emblem of
'ancient Music.

'On the Left (but within the Partition for *Physic*)
'*Dramatic Poesy*, with a Vizard, representing *Comedy*,
'a bloody Dagger for *Tragedy*, and the Reed Pipe for
'*Pastoral*.

'In the Square, on the Right Side of the Circle,
'is *Law*, with her Ruling Scepter, accompanied with
'Records, Patents, and Evidences on the one Side,
'and on the other with *Rhetoric*: by these is an attend-
'ing *Genius*, with the Scales of *Justice*, and a Figure

' with a Palm-branch, the Emblem of Reward for vir-
' tuous actions; and the *Roman Fasces*, the Marks of
' Power and Punishment.
' *Printing*, with a Case of Letters in one Hand,
' and a Form ready set in the other, and by her seve-
' ral sheets hanging to dry.
' On the Left Side the Circle, opposite to *Theology*,
' in three Squares, are the *Mathematical Sciences*, (de-
' pending on *Demonstration*, as the other on *Faith*), in
' the first of which is *Astronomy* with the Celestial Globe,
' *Geography* with the Terrestrial, together with three
' attending *Genii*; having *Arithmetic* in the Square on
' one Hand, with a Paper of Figures; *Optics* with the
' Perspective-glass; *Geometry* with a Pair of Compasses
' in her Left; and a Table with *Geometrical Figures*
' in it, in her Right-hand. And in the Square on the
' other Hand, *Architecture* embracing the Capital of a
' Column, with Compasses, and the Norma or Square
' lying by her, and a Workman holding another Square
' in one Hand, and a Plumb-Line in the other.
' In the midst of these Squares and Triangles (as
' descending from above) is the Figure of *Truth* sitting
' as on a Cloud, in one Hand holding a Palm Branch
' (the Emblem of Victory) in the other the Sun, whose
' Brightness enlightens the whole Circle of Figures, and
' is so bright, that it seems to hide the Face of herself
' to the Spectators below
' Over the Entrance of the Front of the THEATRE,
' are Three Figures tumbling down; First *Envy*, with
' her Snaky Hairs, Squint Eyes, Hag's Breast, pale
' venomous Complexion, strong but ugly limbs, and
' rivel'd Skin, frighted from above by the Sight of the
' Shield of *Pallas*, with the *Gorgon*'s Head in it, against
' which she opposes her snaky Tresses, but her Fall
' is so precipitous, that she has no Command of her
' Arms.
' Then *Rapine*, with her fiery Eyes, grinning Teeth,

' sharp

'sharp Twangs, her Hands imbrued in Blood, holding
a Bloody Dagger in one Hand, in the other a Burning
Flambeau; with these Instruments threatning the
Destruction of Learning, and all its Habitations, but
she is overcome, and prevented, by a *Herculean Genius*, or Power.

'Next that is represented brutish, scoffing Ignorance,
endeavouring to vilify and contemn what she under-
stands not, which is charmed by a *mercurial Genius*
with his *Caduceus*."

In the Theatre are held the Public Acts called the
Comitia, and *Encænia*: At which solemn Times there
are several extraordinary Proctors appointed, who are
to take Care that Public Peace is observed, and that
all Persons are placed according to their Degrees.

This Edifice which justly deserves to be deemed one
of our principal Curiosities, was built by that celebrated Architect Sir *Christopher Wren*, at the Expense of
Archbishop *Sheldon*, the Chancellor, in 1669, and cost
his Grace 15000 *l*. to which he added 2000 *l*. to purchase Lands for the perpetual Repair of it.

On the West of the Theatre is the ASHMOLEAN
MUSEUM, a handsome Edifice, built by the University at the Request of *Elias Ashmole*, Esq; *Windsor* He-
rald to King *Charles* II. who placed here all the Rari-
ties he had collected and purchased, particularly from
the two *Tradescants*. The Building was finished in
1682, under the Conduct of Sir *Christopher Wren*, and
is inferior to none in Symetry and Elegance. The
Eastern Portico is highly finished in the *Corinthian* Order, and adorned with Variety of Characteristical Embellishments.

Mr. *Ashmole* presented to the University a valuable
Collection of Natural Curiosities, Coins, and MSS,
together with three Gold Chains he had received as ho-
norary Presents from the King of *Denmark* and other
Princes on Occasion of his Book on the *Order of the
Garter*. This

This Repository has been greatly enriched by several ample and valuable Benefactions. The principal Natural Curiosities are the Collection of Bodies, Horns, Bones, &c. of Animals preserved dry, or in Spirits; curious and numerous Specimens of Metals and Minerals: Dr. *Lister*'s Collection of Shells, Ores, Fossils, &c. most of which are published in his *Synopsis Conchyliorum*, and in the *Philosophical Transactions*.

Its two first Keepers were Dr. *Robert Plott* and Mr. *Edward Lhuyd*, the former of which deposited here all his Natural Bodies mentioned in his Histories of *Staffordshire* and *Oxfordshire*; and the latter his Collections in his Travels thro' *England*, *Wales*, and *Ireland*, as may be seen in his Book intitled *Lythophylacii Britanici Ichnographia*. Mr. *Borlace*, Author of the *Natural History of Cornwall*, presented to this Museum the Specimens of Chrystals, Mundicks, Coppers, Tins, &c. described in that Work.

The large Magnet, given by the Countess of *Westmorland*, is of an oval Shape, 18 Inches long, 12 wide, and supports a Weight of 145 Pounds.

Three curious Pieces of Art deserve particular Notice, *viz*. a Model of a Ship; a Picture of our Saviour going to his Crucifixion, composed of the most beautiful lively Feathers; and an ancient Piece of St. *Cuthbert*, made by Order of King *Alfred*, and worn as is related by that Monarch.

The last, and very entertaining Present to this Collection, was given by Mr. *Reinhold Forster*, who went the Voyage round the World with Capt. *Cook*, consisting of a great Variety of the Manufactures, Habits, Warlike Instruments, and an Idol, which he brought from the Island of *O-Taheitee* and *New Zealand*.

Among the Paintings are a few very good ones: a *Dead Christ*, by *Hannibal Carrache*. *Thomas* Earl of *Arundel*, and the Duke of *Norfolk*, his Son, by *Vandyke*. *Christ's Descent into Hell*, by *Brugell*.

In this Building are three small Libraries; the first, called *Ashmole*'s Study, contains his printed Books and Manuscripts relating to Heraldry and Antiquity, and the Manuscripts of Sir *William Dugdale*, Author of the *Monasticon Anglicanum*:—The second contains Dr. *Lister*'s Library. The third that of Mr. *Anthony à Wood*, with his laborious and learned Collections, relating chiefly to this University and City.

On the first Floor the Professor reads Lectures in Experimental Philosophy; and underneath is an Elaboratory for Courses of Chemistry and Anatomy.

On the other Side of the Theatre, and North of the Schools, stands the *Clarendon* PRINTING HOUSE, built in the Year 1711, with the Profits arising from the Sale of Lord *Clarendon*'s History; the Copy of which was given to the University by the Lords *Clarendon* and *Rochester*, Sons of that noble Lord. It is a grand Edifice, 115 Feet in Length; and consists of two lofty Stories. Towards the Street is a magnificent *Portico* in the *Doric* Order; the Height of the Columns being equal to the two Stories. This is answered on the opposite Side, next the Schools, by a Frontispiece supported by Three-Quarter Columns of the same Dimensions; and the Doric Entablature encompasses the whole Building. On the Top, are Statues of the Nine Muses; and over the Entrance on the South Side a Statue of the Earl of *Clarendon*. As we enter on this Side, on the Right-hand, are the Apartments where Bibles and Common Prayer Books are printed, under the Privilege and Appointment of the University. On the Left is the University Press; and a well-finished Apartment, where the Heads of Houses and Delegates meet on the Business of the University. In it is a celebrated Portrait of Queen *Anne* by Sir *Godfrey Kneller*.

Southward of the Schools, in the Centre of a beautiful *Area*, adorned with a considerable Number of Obelisks licks and Lamps, stands the new Public Library; for the building whereof, that celebrated Physician Dr. *John Radcliffe* bequeathed the Sum of 40,000*l*. He fixed the Sallary of the Librarian at 150*l. per Annum*; appropriated 100*l. per Annum* to buy Books, and 100*l. per Annum* to keep the Library in Repair.

The Rustic Basement, which is 100 Feet in Diameter from Outside to Outside, is a double Octagon or 16 Square; either of which Squares are distinguished by their Projection, and having over each a Pediment or Frontispiece which forms them into Gate-ways.

The Superstructure, raised upon this Basement, is perfectly *Cylindrical*, and adorned with Three-Quarter Columns of the *Corinthian* Order; which are ranged, not at equal Distances, but in Couplets. Between these, there is an Alternacy of Windows and Niches all round: over the latter, next to the *Architrave*, are beautiful Festoons of Fruits and Flowers. The Entablature is much enriched with Carving; and over it is a Ballustrade surrounding the whole, finished with Vases on the Piers perpendicular to the Columns. Above which is a Cupola, 60 Feet high. Seven of the Gateways abovementioned are Entrances into the *Portico* or *Arcade*; in the Center of which within the Piers is a wide spreading Dome; and without them, a Cloyster almost encircling it. Over each of the Entrances is a Dome of smaller Dimensions, curiously wrought with variety of *Mosaic*. The Eighth Gateway is appropriated to the Stair-case, the Well of which is Oval; the Steps, which are of Stone, easy of Ascent, adhering to the Wall at one End, but seem rather to be upheld by the Iron Rail that is upon them, than supported underneath at the other: This is deemed a curious Piece of Masonry. The Awe we are struck with at entering into the Grand *Area* of the Library, we leave to the Experience of those who feel it; as it is not easily described. The Pavement is of different coloured Stone, brought from

from *Harts Forest* in *Germany*. The Piers or Butments of the Arches are adorned with Pilasters of the *Ionic* Order.

The Dome, which is 80 Feet high from the Pavement, is wrought in curious Compartments in Stucco. It is chiefly lighted by Windows in the Cylindric Part thereof; between which are Tresses of Fruits and Flowers. In the circular Part, without the Piers, are the Book-cases and Reading-tables: This Part is lighted by the small square Windows; which are thus proportioned and disposed, to admit of a Gallery above, which would otherwise have been too high. This Gallery is appropriated to the same Uses as the circular Part beneath. Over the Door is a very good Statue of the Founder by *Rysbrack*: The best point to view it from, is, directly opposite to it, in the Gallery. Over the Entrance of one of the Galleries is a Bust of *Gibbs*, the Architect. The first Stone of this superb Building was laid *May* 17, A. D. 1737; and being compleatly finished, it was opened on *Thursday*, *April* 13, 1749; when the Duke of *Beaufort*, one of the Trustees, delivered the Keys into the Hands of the then Vice-Chancellor, who, in the Name of the University, returned Thanks to the Trustees.

In this Library are a couple of superb Roman Candlesticks, of incomparable Workmanship, given to the University by Sir *Roger Newdigate*, Bart. Their want of similarity adds to their Worth, as by it we have the Benefit of more of the Ingenuity of the Roman Artists. They were found in the Ruins of the Emperor *Adrian's* Palace at *Tivoli*, in the *Campania Romana*.

The Public are indebted to Dr. *Radcliffe's* Trustees for the building and compleatly furnishing the PUBLIC INFIRMARY at the North Side of the City, which is maintained and supported by voluntary Contributions from every Part of the Kingdom, and is distinguished

guished by the Stile of *The President and Governors of the Radcliffe Infirmary, for the Relief of the Sick and Lame Poor, from whatever County recommended.* An institution which in this Place must be productive of very extensive Benefits, as, while it relieves the Poor, it serves for a School for the Students in Physic.

The same munificent Trustees of Dr. *Radcliffe*'s Will, to whom the Public in general, and this Place in particular, are so greatly indebted, have built a magnificent

ASTRONOMICAL OBSERVATORY, far exceeding any other Building for that learned and useful Purpose. It is erected in an open, elevated Place, a little North of the Infirmary, containing about ten Acres. The Ground was a Benefaction of his Grace the Duke of *Marlborough*. The Situation completely advantageous, and not incommoded by the Town. The Execution of the Observatory will be a lasting Honour to Mr. *Wyat*, the celebrated Architect.

After the Public Buildings, a Description of the PHYSIC GARDEN properly follows. It is situated on the South of *Magdalene* College. This was the Donation of *Henry D'Anvers*, Earl of *Danby*, who purchased the Ground (containing five Acres) of *Magdalene* College, surrounded it with a lofty Wall, and erected, next to the Street, a parapet with Iron Palisades thereon. The Piers which support these and the other Iron-work, being properly ornamented with *Vases* of Fruits and Flowers of various Kinds, serving as a Fence to the Green-Court, through which we pass to the Gate-way.

This Gate-way is justly esteemed an elegant Piece of Architecture. The Design is ascribed to *Inigo Jones*; nor is it unworthy of that Architect. The manner of it is thus: It is of the *Doric* Proportion, but without Triglyphs. The Columns and other Parts of the Building are

are curiously wrought with *Ruſtic*. The Frontiſpiece
conſiſts of two ſmall Pediments, and one of larger Dimenſion; which, at its Extremities, partly covers the
other two. In the Center over the Arch is a Buſt of
the Founder, Lord *Danby*. On the Left-hand of the
Entrance is a Statue of CHARLES I. and on the Right-hand, one of CHARLES II. The Niches in which theſe
ſtand are finiſhed by the two ſmall Pediments abovementioned. On the Face of the *Corona* and the *Frize*
is the following Inſcription; viz. *Gloriæ Dei optimi
maximi Honori Caroli* I. *Regis in Uſum Academiæ & Reipublicæ* Henricus *Comes* Danby, *Anno* 1632. This Inſcription is likewiſe on the Garden Front.

The Garden is divided into four Quarters, with a
broad Walk down the Middle, a croſs Walk, and one
all round. Near the Entrance, are two elegant and
uſeful *Green-Houſes*, one on the Right, the other on the
Left, built by the Univerſity for *Exotics*; of which
there is a conſiderable Collection. In the Quarters,
within the Yew Hedges, is the greateſt Variety of ſuch
Plants as require no artificial Heat to nouriſh them, all
ranged in the proper Claſſes, and numbered.

Eaſtward of the Garden, without the Walls, is an
excellent Hot-houſe; where tender Plants, ſuch whoſe
native Soil lies between the Tropics, are raiſed and
brought to great Perfection; viz. the Anana or Pine-Apple, the Plantain, the Coffee Shrub, the Caper Tree,
the Cinnamon, the Creeping Cereus, and many others.
Theſe Pine-Apples have nearly the ſame Flavour as
thoſe raiſed in warmer Climates; the Caper and the
Coffee Shrub alſo bear well.

This uſeful Foundation has been much improved by
the late Dr. *Sherard*, who brought from *Smyrna* a valuable Collection of Plants. He built the Library adjoining to the Garden, and furniſhed it with a curious Collection of Botanical Books, and a valuable *Hortus Siccus*.
The Eaſt End of this Building is the Apartment for

the Profeſſor, whoſe Salary is paid out of the Intereſt of 3000*l.* given by Dr. *Sherard* for that Purpoſe. The Aſſiſtant to the Profeſſor is provided by the Univerſity.

We proceed next to deſcribe and give ſome Account of the ſeveral Colleges; and as *Magdalen* College is the neareſt to the Place we laſt mentioned, and the firſt we meet with in the Road from *London,* it may not be improper to begin with that.

MAGDALEN College.

THE College of St. *Mary Magdalen* is ſituated upon the River *Cherwell,* near the Phyſic-Garden. The firſt Thing worthy the Attention of a curious Obſerver, is the Weſt Entrance into the Chapel; over which are five ſmall hiſtorical Figures, of elegant Sculpture. That on the Right, in a kneeling Poſture, repreſents the *Founder*; the next *William of Wickham,* the Founder of the two St. *Mary Winton* Colleges; that in the Middle, St. *Mary Magdalen,* to whom the College is dedicated; the next, in a kneeling Poſture, King *Henry* III. who founded the Hoſpital which was converted into this College; and that on the Left, St. *John the Baptiſt,* to whom the ſaid Hoſpital was dedicated.

The Building on the Left-hand is the Preſident's Lodgings; adjoining to which is a magnificent Gothic Gate-way (formerly the Grand Entrance into the College) adorned with Statues as large as the Life, of four of the above Perſons, viz. the *Founder,* St *Mary Magdalen,* King *Henry* III. and St. *John the Baptiſt.*

Between the Chapel and the above Gate-way we enter the Cloyſter; near this Entrance is the Chapel, which is a well-proportioned Edifice in form of a *Roman* T inverted. The Ante-Chapel is remarkable for it's elegant Monuments; particularly one, on the Left-hand

of the Organ-loft, erected to the Memory of Two Brothers of the Name of *Lyttleton*, who were drowned in the River *Cherwell*, one by endeavouring to save the other. The whole of the Ante-Chapel has been lately adorned in an elegant Manner with a new Pulpit, Lecturer's Seat, and new Paving.

The Weſt Window, painted in *Claro Obſcuro*, was done after a Deſign of *Schwartz* which he made and executed for the Princeſs of *William* Duke of *Bavaria*, as appears by a Print lately purchaſed by the Society, engraved by *Sadelar* from the Original. It repreſents the Reſurrection; and, by the Print, was certainly a grand Deſign; but the Beauty of the Painting is much impaired. Till the Time of the Civil Wars, all the Windows were painted in the ſame Manner. Thoſe now in the Chapel were removed thither from the Ante-Chapel in 1741; but not being a ſufficient Number to completely glaze the whole, two new ones have ſince been added.

The Altar-Piece was painted by *Iſaac Fuller*, an *Engliſh* Hiſtory-painter, about 120 Years ago: who having ſtudied and admired the muſcular Manner of *Michael Angelo*, ſeems to have neglected the graceful Elegance of *Raphael*: For although many of the Figures may juſtly be deemed excellent Anatomical or Academy Drawings; yet for want of that eaſy and natural Diſpoſition, peculiar to the laſt-mentioned great Maſter, and better Colouring, the whole appears crude and unpleaſing. This Painting, however, gave occaſion to the Writing of an excellent *Latin* Poem by Mr. *Addiſon*, (ſometime Fellow of this College) which may be ſeen in the *Muſæ Anglicanæ*.

Underneath this Piece of the Reſurrection by *Fuller*, is an admirable Picture of our Saviour bearing his Croſs, ſuppoſed to be painted by *Guido*. It was taken at *Vigo*, and brought into *England* by the late Duke of *Ormond*: But afterwards falling into the Hands of *William Free-*

man, Efq; of *Hamels* in *Hertfordshire*, he gave it to the College. To this Gentleman the College is likewise chiefly obliged for an excellent Organ, two additional Bells to the Peal of Eight, and other confiderable Benefactions. By his Will he bequeathed an Organ, which then ftood at *Hamels*, to the *Mufic-Room* in *Oxford*, provided there fhould be no Inftrument of that Kind in it at the Time of his Death; otherwife to be erected in the Hall belonging to this College: But the former happening to be the Cafe, it accordingly went thither; for which the Public and Mufical Society are obliged to him.

The Altar has been built, in the prefent Manner, a few Years only; the Defign is elegant, and the Workmanfhip well performed: Befides the common Embellifhments of the Corinthian Order, there are Feftoons over every Pannel (extremely well carved) which greatly enrich it.

Each Window contains fix Figures, nearly as large as the Life, reprefenting the Apoftles, primitive Fathers, Saints and Martyrs. Many think this Room rather too dark at firft entering it, but afterwards are better reconciled: The Occafion of that Opinion is, undoubtedly, the Contraft between this and the Ante-Chapel, which they pafs through to it, and which is extremely light. Cathedral Service is performed here every Day at Ten and Four, except *Sundays* and Holidays, and then the Morning Prayers begin at Eight, on Account of the Univerfity Sermon.

From hence, on the Right, we pafs into the Cloyfter which encompaffes the great Quadrangle, and remains in it's primitive State: The whole making the moft venerable Appearance of any College in *Oxford*, having undergone the feweft Alterations of any fince it was founded. On the South Side are the Hall and Chapel; on the Weft the Library; and on the North and Eaft, the Lodgings of the Fellows, Demies, &c. At the

South-

South-east Corner of the Cloyster, is the Way up to
the Hall; which is a very spacious Room, handsomely
fitted up, and adorned with four whole length Pourtraits, viz. of the *Founder*, Dr. *Butler* the late President, *William Freeman*, Esq; and Prince *Rupert*; two
Half-lengths, viz. Bishop *Warner*, a great Benefactor
to the Library, and Dr. *Hammond*.

The interiour Part of this Quadrangle is ornamented
with Hieroglyphics, of which, (though a celebrated
Antiquary * hath been pleased to call them *whimsical
Figures, which serve to amuse the Vulgar, but are only the
licentious Inventions of the Mason,*) we shall here give a
particular, and, we trust, a rational Account, from a
Latin † Manuscript in the Library of this College.

' Beginning, therefore, from the South-west Corner,
' the two first Figures we meet with are the *Lion,* and
' the *Pelican.* The former of these is the Emblem of
' *Courage* and *Vigilance,* the latter of *parental Tenderness,
' and Affection.* Both of them together express to us
' the complete Character of a good Governor of a
' College. Accordingly they are placed under the
' Window of those Lodgings, which, originally, be-
' longed to the President, as the Instructions they con-
' vey ought particularly to regulate his Conduct.

' Going on to the right Hand, on the other Side of
' the Gate-way, are four Figures, viz. the *School-master,*
' the *Lawyer,* the *Physician,* and the *Divine.* These are
' ranged along the Outside of the Library, and repre-

---

* See Dr. *Stukeley*'s Itinerarium Curiosum, p. 42.

† This Piece is intituled *Oedipus Magdalenensis: Explicatio viz.
Imaginum, & Figurarum, quæ apud Magdalenenses in interiori Collegii
Quadrangulo Tibicinibus impositæ visuntur.* It was written by Mr.
William Reeks, sometime Fellow of this College, at the Request of
Dr. *Clark,* who was President from the Year 1671, to 1687, and to
whom it is inscribed. It is divided into two Parts. In the first, the
general Doctrine of Hieroglyphics is very learnedly discussed. In the
latter, he descends to a particular Consideration of the Hieroglyphics
at *Magdalen;* and from this Part the Account here given is extracted.

'sent the Duties and Business of the Students of the
'House. By means of Learning in general, they are
'to be introduced to one of the three learned Profes-
'sions, or else as hinted to us by the Figure with *Cap* and
'*Bells* in the Corner, they must turn out *Fools* in the End.
 'We come now to the North Side of the Quadran-
'gle, and here the three first Figures represent the
'History of *David*, his Conquest over the *Lion* and
'*Goliah*; from whence we are taught, not to be dif-
'couraged at any Difficulties that may stand in our
'Way, as the *Vigour of Youth* will easily enable us to
'surmount them. The next Figure to these is that of
'the *Hippopotamos*, or *River-Horse*, carrying his young
'one upon his Shoulders. This is the Emblem of a
'good Tutor, or Fellow of a College, who is set to
'watch over the Youth of the Society, and by whose
'Prudence they are to be led through the Dangers of
'their first Entrance into the World. The Figure im-
'mediately following represents *Sobriety*, or *Temperance*,
'that most necessary Virtue of a Collegiate Life. The
'whole remaining Train of Figures are the Vices we
'are instructed to avoid. Those next to Temperance
'are the opposite Vices of *Gluttony* and *Drunkenness*.
'Then follow the *Lucanthropos*, the *Hyæna*, and *Pan-
'ther*, representing *Violence*, *Fraud*, and *Treachery*; the
'*Gryphin* representing *Covetousness*, and the next Figure
'*Anger*, or *Moroseness*. The *Dog*, the *Dragon*, the *Deer*,
'*Flattery*, *Envy*, and *Timidity*; and the three last, the
'*Manticbora*, the *Baxers*, and the *Lamia*, *Pride*, *Conten-
'tion*, and *Lust*.
 'We have here, therefore, a complete and instruc-
'tive Lesson, for the Use of a Society dedicated to
'the Advancement of Religion and Learning; and,
'on this Plan, we may suppose the Founder of *Magda-
'len* thus speaking, by means of these Figures, to the
'Students of his College.
 "It is your Duty, who live under the Care of a
"President,

"President, whose *Vigilance*, and *Parental Tenderness*, are the proper Qualifications to support the Government of my House, attentively to pursue your Studies, in your *several Professions*; and so to avoid the *Follies* of an idle, unlettered, and dissipated Course of Life. You may possibly meet with many *Difficulties*, at your first setting out in this Road, but these every *Stripling* will be able to overcome by *Courage* and *Perseverance*. And remember, when you are advanced beyond these Difficulties, that it is your Duty to lend your Assistance to those who come after you, and whose Education is committed to your Care. You are to be an Example to them of *Sobriety*, and *Temperance*: So shall you guard them from falling into the Snares of *Excess*, and *Debauchery*. You shall teach them that the Vices with which the World abounds, *Cruelty*, *Fraud*, *Avarice*, *Anger* and *Envy*, as well as the more supple ones of abject *Flattery*, and *Cowardice*, are not to be countenanced within these hallowed Retirements. And let it be your Endeavour to avoid *Pride* and *Contention*, the Parents of Faction, and, in your Situation, the worst and most unnatural of all Factions, the *Faction of a Cloyster*. And lastly, you will complete the *Collegiate Character*, if you crown all your other Acquirements with the unspotted *Purity*, and *Chastity*, of your Lives and Conversation."

' We hope, by this Time, the Reader is convinced, that so exact a System of Morals, could not easily have been produced from the *licentious Inventions of the Mason*.'

From the Cloyster we go through a narrow Passage in the North Side, into the Court where the New Building stands. This Edifice is 300 Feet in Length, and consists of three Stories above the Cellars, besides the Garrets. This Front is supported by an *Arcade*, which forms a beautiful Cloyster. The whole is built of *Heddington*

dington Stone, and is juftly deemed an elegant Structure. It has confiderably the Advantage of fome other modern Buildings; for whereas the *upper Story* of thofe is commonly an *Attic*, and confequently the Rooms lower than thofe of the *middle Story*; the Rooms in the upper Story here are exactly of the fame Dimenfion with thofe below; and command a better Profpect. Three other Sides were intended to be added; but probably fince the Effect of that beautiful Opening to the Meadow has been feen, * the Society may think proper, in fome Refpect, to alter their Defign.

One unparalleled Beauty belonging to this College is the extenfive Out-let. The Grove feems perfectly adapted to indulge Contemplation; being a pleafant Kind of Solitude, laid out in Walks, and well planted with Trees. It has in it about forty Head of Deer.

Befide the Walks which are in the Grove there is a very delightful, and much frequented one, round a Meadow containing about thirteen Acres, furrounded by the feveral Branches of the *Cherwell*; from whence it is called the *Water-Walks*; which yields all the Variety that could be wifhed: Some Parts of it running in ftraight Lines, with the Trees formerly more regularly cut than at prefent; others winding, and the Trees growing little otherwife than as Nature directs: There is plenty of Water as well as Verdure, and an agreeable View of the Country adjacent.

This College was founded by *William Patten*, called WILLIAM of WAINFLEET, from a Village of that Name in *Lincolnfhire*, where he was born. He was educated at *Winchefter* School, and was afterwards Fellow of *New College* in *Oxford*. Having taken the Degree of Bachelor of Divinity, he was appointed chief Mafter of *Winchefter* School, where he continued 12 Years, and then was made School-mafter, and foon after Provoft of *Eton* College by King *Henry* VI. who preferred

* See the Perfpective View annexed.

him

him to the Bishopric of *Winchester* in the Year 1447, and in 1449 he was constituted Lord High Chancellor of *England*.

He first founded a Hall in *Oxford* without the East Gate, which he dedicated to the Honour of St. *Mary Magdalen*, and in the Year 1456 obtained Leave of King *Henry* VI. to convert St. *John*'s Hospital, situated further Eastward, into a College. It consists of a President, forty Fellows, thirty Demies, a Divinity Lecturer, School-master, and Usher, four Chaplains, an Organist, eight Clerks, and sixteen Choristers. The whole Number of Students, including Gentlemen Commoners, is about 120.

It was customary on St. *John Baptist*'s Day to have the University-Sermon preached in the Stone Pulpit at the South-east Corner of the first Court within the College Gate; which on that Occasion was decked with Boughs and Rushes, alluding to St. *John*'s preaching in the Wilderness.

The last Thing we shall take Notice of, is the Tower. This was erected by the College under the Direction of Cardinal *Wolsey*, who was Fellow, (and at that Time) Bursar of this College. It is about 150 Feet high, and by it's solid and substantial Basis, Number of Set-offs, and gradual Diminution, is calculated for Strength and Duration.

The most advantageous View of it, is from the Physic Garden. We must not omit mentioning that this Tower contains a very musical Peal of Ten Bells; and that on *May* Day Morning, the Clerks and Choristers assemble on the Top of it, and instead of a Mass of Requiem for King *Henry* VII. sing chearful Songs and Catches.

Visitor, The Bishop of *Winchester*.

Queen's

QUEEN's COLLEGE.

ON the North Side of the *High-Street*, opposite *University* College, is *Queen's* College.

The whole Area, on which this fine College is built, is an oblong Square, of 300 Feet in Length, and 220 in Breadth, which being divided by the Hall and Chapel forms two spacious Courts.

The South End, which is the grand Front, abuts upon the *High-Street*, in the Middle whereof is a magnificent Gate, and over it the Statue of Queen *Caroline*, under a Cupola supported by Pillars; the rest of the Front being adorned with Niches; but no Chambers on this Side, except at each End.

The first, or South Court, is a handsome Quadrangle, 140 Feet long, and 130 broad, having a lofty Cloister, supported by square Pillars, on the West, South, and East. Over the West Cloister are two Stories, consisting of the Chambers of the Fellows and Students, an elegant Gallery, and Common Room, and in that Cloister is the Apartment of the Provost. Over the East Cloister are also Chambers for the Fellows and Students, and some for those of the late Benefaction of Mr. *Michell*. The second, or North Court, has the Library over it on the West, and Chambers for the Fellows and Students on the North, East, and South.

The Chapel is 100 Feet long, and 30 broad. In the arched Roof is a Piece of Painting by Sir *James Thornhill*. The Windows are admirably painted; the Subject of that over the Altar, by Mr. *Price* in 1717, is the Nativity of our Saviour. The Side Windows were removed thither from the old Chapel: two on the North Side are the last Judgment, and two others on the South, the Afcenfion. The reft are all of old Glafs, remarkable for the Livelinefs of the Colours.

There is a Paffage between the Chapel and the Hall from the South to the North Court, the Walls of which carry a handfome Cupola with eight Ionic Columns, and all the proper Ornaments of that Order. The Outfide of the whole is a Doric Building, and the Infide of the Hall beautified with the fame Order: But the Infide of the Chapel is entirely Corinthian, the Cieling of which is not inferior to the reft.

The Hall is 60 Feet long, and 30 broad, with an arched Roof of a fuitable Height. It is furnifhed with Portraits of the Founder and principal Benefactors; to which has lately been added a good Picture of her prefent Majefty Queen *Charlotte*. It is extremely well illuminated, and has a Chimney Piece of beautiful Marble; and there is an Opening from the Gallery over the Weft Cloifter, which feems defigned for Mufic; and hither Strangers are frequently brought, who defire to fee the Society at Dinner.

The Library on the Weft Side of the North Court, about 123 Feet in Length, is a noble Building of the Corinthian Order, with a fpacious Cloifter to the Eaft, and the Statue of the Founder, and principal Benefactors to the College, in Niches to the Weft, and is adorned with Stucco Work by the late Mr. *Roberts*. It has beautiful Claffes, a fplendid Orrery, and is furnifhed with a valuable Collection of Books and Manufcripts in moft Languages and Sciences. It is alfo ornamented with a high-finifhed Figure of a Wild Boar.

Robert Egglesfield, a Native of *Cumberland*, Confeffor to Queen *Philippa*, and Bachelor of Divinity in this Univerfity, having purchafed feveral Tenements in the Parifh of St. *Peter's* in the *Eaft*, erected there a Collegiate Hall, at the Inftance (and, probably by the Encouragement) of Queen *Philippa*, Confort of King *Edward* III. giving it the Name of *Aula Scholarium*

rium Reginæ de Oxon; and on the 18th of *January* 1340, obtained the Royal Charter for incorporating the Society of this Hall or College; by virtue whereof he constituted a Provost and twelve Fellows, ordering, that the Provost should be chosen out of the Fellows, and be in Holy Orders; and that for the future the Fellows should be elected out of the Counties of *Cumberland* and *Westmorland*.

The principal Benefactors, besides the Founder, were King *Edward* III. and his Queen *Philippa*; King *Charles* I. who gave this College three Rectories and three Vicarages in *Hampshire*; Sir *Joseph Williamson*, Knight, sometime Fellow, who rebuilt Part of the College, and left 6000*l.* towards the finishing of it, besides a most valuable Library of Books; Dr. *Barlow*, Bishop of *Lincoln*; Dr. *Lancaster*, the Provost of this College, and Dr. *Timothy Halton*, were great Benefactors. And of late several very considerable Exhibitions have been given by Sir *Francis Bridgman*, Lady *Elizabeth Hastings*, and Mr. *Michell* of *Richmond*.

The Members in this College are a Provost, sixteen Fellows, two Chaplains, eight Taberdars, (so called from *Taberdum*, a short gown which they formerly wore) 16 Scholars, two Clerks, and forty Exhibitioners; Mr. *Michell*'s eight Fellows, and four Scholars; besides a great Number of Masters, Bachelors, Gentlemen Commoners, Commoners, and other Students; in all about 110.

A Custom here is, that they are call'd to Dinner and Supper by the Sound of the Trumpet, and the Fellows, as the Founder's Statutes direct, place themselves on the further Side of the Table, the Taberdars on *Sundays* and Holidays dispute on some of the most controverted Questions in Divinity; and on other Days render some Parts of *Aristotle*'s Rhetoric, Poetics, or Ethics.

Another Custom is, that the Bursar of the College, on *New-Year*'s Day, gives each Member a Needle and Thread,

Thread, faying, *Take ibis, and be thrifty*, as a Rebus on the Founder's Name *(Aiguile)* in French, fignifying a Needle, and *Fil*, a Thread, *Egglesfield*.

Another is, having a Boar's Head on *Chriftmas* Day, ufher'd in very folemnly with a celebrated Monkifh Song.

   Vifitor. The Archbifhop of *York*.

UNIVERSITY College.

OPPOSITE *Queen's*, on the South Side of the *High Street*, ftands *Univerfity* College. The magnificent Front extends 260 Feet. In it, at proper Diftances, are two Portals, with a Tower over each. That on the Weft leads into the old Court, which is a handfome Gothic Quadrangle, of 100 Feet fquare. Over the Gate, at our Entrance, on the Outfide, is a Statue of Queen *Anne*, and within another of *James* II. Over the Eaftern Entrance, on the Outfide, is a Statue of Queen *Mary*, Wife of *William* III. On the South of the Weftern Quadrangle are the Chapel and Hall. The Statue of St. *Cuthbert* is over the Door of the Chapel. The Altar Window was given by Dr. *Radcliffe*, as appears by its Infcription, A. D. 1667, the other Windows are of fine old Painted Glafs, well worthy Attention. The Roof of the Chapel is a well-wrought Frame of *Norway* Oak. The Hall, at the Entrance of which is a Statue of King *Alfred*, has been lately fitted up in a very beautiful Gothic Style, at the Expenfe of many generous Contributors, and is a moft complete Room of the Kind.

From this Court, through a narrow Paffage on the Eaft, we are led into another Area of three Sides, 80 Feet either Way. It is opened to a Garden on the South. The Eaft, and Part of the North Side, is taken up by the Lodgings of the Master, which are commodious and extensive. In a Niche over the Gate on the North, is a Statue of Dr. *Radcliffe*.

King *Alfred* in the Year 872, erected certain Halls in *Oxford*, near, or on the Spot where this College stands; and gave the Students in them small Pensions issuing from the Exchequer. But it is certain that these Halls were soon alienated to the Citizens, and that their Pensions were suppressed about the Reign of the Conqueror. The Founder of this College appears to be *William* Archdeacon of *Durham*, who purchasing, A.D. 1219, one of the Halls which had been originally erected by King *Alfred*, and very probably styled *University* Hall, of the Citizens, endowed it with Lands. A Society being thus established, many other Benefactors improved the Revenues and Buildings. Of these the most considerable are *Walter Skirlow*, Bishop of *Durham*, who founded three Fellowships. *Henry Piercy* Earl of *Northumberland*, A.D. 1443, added the same Number. Sir *Simon Bennet*, in the Reign of *Charles* I. established four Fellowships, and four Scholarships.

As to the Buildings, the present spacious and uniform Structure began to be erected, A.D. 1634, by the Benefaction of *Charles Greenwood*, formerly Fellow, and was soon carried on by Sir *Simon Bennet* abovementioned. Nor were succeeding Patrons wanting to continue so noble a Work; till it was finally compleated by Dr. *John Radcliffe*, who erected the whole Eastern Quadrangle at his own Expense. He settled on the College 600 *l. per Annum*, for two travelling Fellowships, Students in Physic, to improve themselves in the Medical Art.

The present Society consists of a Master, twelve Fellows, seventeen Scholars, with many other Students, amounting in the whole to about 70.

Visitor, The K i n g.

ALL-

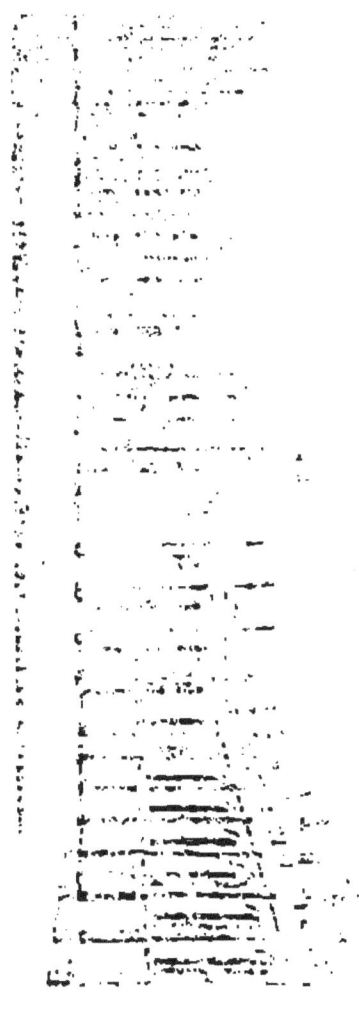

PART OF ALL SOULS COLLEGE.

ALL-SOULS College.

THIS College is situated West of *Queen*'s, and consists chiefly of two Courts. 1. The old Court is about 124 Feet in Length, and 72 in Breadth, having the *High-Street* on the South, and the Chapel at the North End of it. In this old Quadrangle is a Dial, contrived by that ingenious Architect Sir *Christopher Wren*, when Fellow of the College, which, by the Help of two Half Rays, and one whole One for every Hour, shews to a Minute what is the Time, the Minutes being mark'd on the Sides of the Rays, fifteen on each Side, and divided in five by a different Character.

2. Their grand Court, situated behind the former, is a spacious and beautiful Quadrangle, having the Library on the North, the Hall and Chapel on the South, the Cloister on the West, and the Common Room, with other handsome Apartments, on the East, adorned with two beautiful *Gothic* Towers. This Court is in Length from North to South about 172 Feet, and in Breadth 155. The Chapel of this College is about 70 Feet long, and 30 broad; the Ante-Chapel of the same Dimensions; the Altar-Piece is of a beautiful clouded Marble, and over it a fine Assumption-Piece of the Founder, painted by Sir *James Thornhill*. Here are also two elegant Vases, One on each Side of the Altar, by the same Hand; the Bas-relief of which represents the Institution of the Two Sacraments. The Compartment over the Communion Table is filled with a Picture painted at *Rome* in the Year 1771, by the celebrated Mr. *Mengs*. The Subject of this Piece is our Saviour's first Appearance to *Mary Magdalen* after his Resurrection; which is called, by the Painters, a *Noli me tangere*, in Allusion to the first Words of *Christ*'s Speech to her, "*Touch me not.*" The Colouring is exquisite;

especially in the Body of our Saviour. There is something very amiable, mixed with dignity, in the Countenance and Character of this Figure; while the mild Composure of it is finely contrasted by that Extasy of Joy and Astonishment which appears on the Face of *Mary*.

The Roof of the Chapel is divided into Compartments, carved and gilded. The Screen, which divides the Chapel from the Ante-Chapel, is a neat Piece of Architecture by Sir *Christopher Wren*.

The New Library is a magnificent Gallery, 200 Feet long, and 30 broad, and about 40 Feet high, built of white hewn Stone, and finished at a great Expense. The Outside is *Gothic*, in Conformity with the rest of the Quadrangle. The Inside consists of two grand Ranges of Bookcases, one above the other, supported by Pilasters of the *Doric* and *Ionic* Orders. Over the Bookcases are placed interchangeably Vases and Bustoes of many eminent Persons, formerly Fellows of this Society.

The following is an exact List of the Busts, beginning on the South Side of the West Window, viz.

1. Sir *Anthony Shirley*, Knight, A. B. Count of the Empire, and Embassador from *Sebach Abbas* Emperor of *Persia*, to the *Christian* Princes; in the Reign of *James* I. admitted Fellow 1582.

2. Sir *William Petre*, Knight, LL. D. Secretary of State to *Henry* VIII. and *Edward* VI. and Privy Counsellor to Queen *Mary* and Queen *Elizabeth*, 1523.

3. *George Clarke*, LL. D. Secretary of War, and afterwards, in the Reign of Queen *Anne*, one of the Lords of the Admiralty, Secretary to Prince of *George* of *Denmark*, and in five Parliaments Burgess for the University, 1680.

4. Sir *Daniel Dunn*, Knight, LL. D. Dean of the Arches, and one of the first Burgesses in Parliament for the University, 1567.

5. *Henry Coventry*, Esq; LL. B. Embassador at *Paris*, and Secretary of State in the Reign of *Charles* II. 1634.

6. Sir *Robert Weston*, Knight, LL. D. Dean of the Arches, and Lord Chancellor of *Ireland*, 1536.

7. Sir *William Trumbull*, Knight, LL. D. Embassador to the *French* and *Turkish* Courts in the Reign of *James* II. Secretary of State to King *William* III. and Burgess of the University. 1657.

8. *Charles Talbot*, LL. D. Baron of *Henfol*, and Lord High Chancellor of *England*, 1704.

9. Sir *Christopher Wren*, Knight, the famous Architect, LL. D. and Savilian Professor of Astronomy, 1653.

10. *Richard Steward*, LL. D. Dean of St. *Paul*'s, Provost of *Eton*, Clerk of the Closet to *Charles* I. and Commissioner for Ecclesiastical Affairs at the Treaty at *Uxbridge*, 1613.

11. *Thomas Tanner*, D. D. Bishop of St. *Asaph*, 1696.

12. *James Goldwell*, LL. D. Bishop of *Norwich*, and Secretary of State to *Edward* IV. 1441.

13. *Gilbert Sheldon*, D. D. Archbishop of *Canterbury*, and Chancellor of the University, 1622.

14. *Brian Duppa*, D. D. Bishop of *Winchester*, Preceptor to *Charles* II. when Prince of *Wales*, and Lord Almoner, 1612.

15. *David Pole*, LL. D. Dean of the Arches and Bishop of *Peterborough*, 1520.

16. *Jeremy Taylor*, D. D. Bishop of *Down* and *Connor*, 1635.

17. *John Norris*, A. M. Rector of *Bemerton*, *Wilts*, 1680.

18. *Thomas Sydenham*, M D. 1648.

19. *Thomas Lynaker*, M. D. Founder of the College of Physicians, *London*, 1484.

20. Sir *Clement Edmonds*, Knight, A. M. Secretary of the Council, in the Reign of *James* I. and Burgess for the University, 1590.

21. Sir *William Byrde*, Knight, LL. D. Dean of the Arches and Burgess for the University, 1578.

22. Sir *Nathaniel Lloyd*, Knight, LL. D. Judge Advocate, and Master of *Trinity Hall* in *Cambridge*, 1689.
23. *Robert Hovenden*, D. D. Warden of *All-Souls*, 1565.
24. Sir *John Mason*, Knight, M. D. Privy Counsellor to *Henry* VIII. *Edward* VI. Queen *Mary*, and Queen *Elizabeth*, and the first Lay Chancellor of the University of *Oxford*, 1521.

Over the great Door is a very fine Bust of the Founder, Archbishop *Chichely*, in white Marble, done by Mr. *Roubiliac*. The Elegance of the Room, and the Choiceness of the Collection, consisting greatly of scarce and foreign Books, make this esteemed one of the best Libraries in *Oxford*.

The Statue of that generous Benefactor, Colonel *Codrington*, is erected in the Middle of the Library, on a Pedestal of veined Marble; this Part of the Building being twice the Breadth of the rest. It appears by an Inscription on the Pedestal, that the Colonel died *Anno* 1710, and that the Statue was erected in 1730. The Area, or wide Space in the Middle of the Building, divides it in a manner into two Rooms.

The Hall is an elegant Room, in which are the Portraits of Archbishop *Chichely*, Founder; Colonel *Codrington*, and Sir *Nathaniel Lloyd*. At the upper End of the Room, under the Founder's Picture, is a Piece of Sir *James Thornhill*'s representing the Finding of the Law, and *Josiah* renting his Cloaths, from 2 *Kings* xxii. 11. Over the Chimney-piece, which is a very neat one of Dove-coloured Marble, is a Bust of the Founder, and on one Side of him *Lynaker*, and on the other *John Leland*, the famous Antiquarian and Author of the Itinerary; who, as Mr. *Hearne* informs us, was a Member of this Society. This Room is ornamented with many other Busts, which are chiefly Copies from antique Originals. The

The College Buttery, which is divided by a Paſſage from the Hall, is a very pretty Room, of an oval Form, with an arch'd Stone Roof of very curious Work.

The Common Room is a very good One, being a Cube of 26 Feet, and lighted by a large Venetian Window.

The Warden's Lodgings, which front the *High-Street*, and are contiguous to the reſt of the College, is a handſome Houſe, late the Dwelling of *George Clarke*, LL. D. a great Benefactor.

The Private Apartments of the College are generally very neat and convenient. The Room in the Old Quadrangle, which was formerly the Library, (before the New one above-deſcribed was finiſhed) is lately fitted up, by one of the Fellows, in a very elegant Manner, in the *Gothic* Taſte; and is deſervedly eſteemed one of the Curioſities of the Houſe.

The Founder of this College, Dr. *Henry Chichely*, was born at *Higham Ferrers* in *Northamptonſhire*; and having had his School Learning in that Town, was, in in the Year 1387, made by *William of Wykeham*, one of his firſt Sett of Fellows at *New College* in *Oxford*, where he took the Degree of Doctor of Civil Law. He was made Archdeacon of *Sarum*, and afterwards Chancellor of the ſame Church; and becoming known to *Henry* IV. was ſent on ſeveral Embaſſies by that Monarch, and advanced firſt to the Biſhopric of St. *David's*, in which having continued five Years, he was tranſlated on *July* 29, 1414, to the See of *Canterbury*, of which he remained Archbiſhop twenty-nine Years. He laid the Foundation of *All Souls* College in 1437; the Charter of Incorporation is dated *May* 20, 16 *Henry* VI. in which it is called *Collegium Animarum omnium Fidelium defunctorum de* Oxon. that is, *The College of the Souls of all Faithful People departed of* Oxford.

By the Statutes he gave this College, he appointed forty Fellows, whereof twenty-four were directed to

ſtudy

study Divinity and Philosophy, and the other sixteen the Civil and Canon Law. He procured from King *Henry* VI. a Grant of the Lands and Revenues of several dissolved Priories to endow his College, and in his Life-time erected the Chapel, and all the rest of the Buildings (except some very modern ones) which cost him 4545 *l.* and at his Death gave to the Society the Sums of 134 *l.* 6 *s.* 8 *d.* and 100 Marks.

The most considerable Benefactors, next to the Founder, have been Colonel *Christopher Codrington*, Governor of the *Leeward Islands*, and Fellow of *All-Souls*, already-mentioned; *George Clarke*, L.L.D. the late Duke of *Wharton*; *Doddington Greville*, Esq; Lieutenant General *Stewart*, and Sir *Nathaniel Lloyd*, who, at the Time that he was Fellow of this College, was Head of of a College in *Cambridge*. The Colonel bequeathed 6000 *l.* for building the noble Library already described, his own valuable Study of Books, and 4000 *l.* more to purchase new ones; and Dr. *Clarke* gave his beauful House, &c. for the Use of the Warden successively of the College. He also much augmented the Chaplainships.

In this College are a Warden, forty Fellows, two Chaplains, and six Clerks.

A very peculiar Custom is the celebrating the *Mallard* Night, every Year, on the 14th of *January*, in Remembrance of an excessive large *Mallard* or *Drake*, supposed to have long rang'd in a Drain or Sewer, where it was found at the Digging for the Foundation of the College. A very authentic Account of this Event hath lately been retrieved, and published to the learned World, from a Manuscript of *Thomas Walsingham* the Historian, and Monk of St. *Alban's*. It is the Cause of much Mirth, for on the Day, and in Remembrance of the *Mallard*, is always sung a merry Old Song set to ancient Music.

Visitor. The Archbishop of *Canterbury*.

BRASE-

BRASE-NOSE College——

FORMS the West Side of the *Radcliffe* Square. Was founded in the Year 1507, by the joint Benefaction of *William Smith*, Bishop of *Lincoln*, and Sir *Richard Sutton*, Knight. Over the Gate are the Arms of the latter.

The most probable Account of the *uncommon Name* of this College seems to be this: The Founders purchased from *University* College, for the Scite of their intended Building, two ancient Seats of Learning, *Brase-Nose* and *Little University* Halls; or, as the last was more commonly call'd, *Black Hall.* Both these are supposed to have received their respective Names from some Students, who removed thither from two such Seminaries in the temporary University of *Stamford*. And *Anthony Wood* says the *Stamford* Seminary was call'd *Brazen-Nose* from an Iron Ring fix'd in a Nose of Brass serving as a Knocker to the Gate; which is said to be remaining there at this Time.

But another Antiquary, Dr. *White Kennet*, says, that it was originally a *Copper-Nose*, or a red Carbuncled-Nose, which was commonly exposed as a Sign to some *Hospitia*, or Houses of Entertainment; and from thence probably, the *Hotel*, or Hall at *Oxford*, as well as the other at *Stamford*, had it's denomination.

The Founders, with a View to both these ancient Seats of Learning, ordered their New Seminary to be called, *The King's Hall and College of Brasen-Nose.* Agreeable to its Antiquity as *University Hall*, there are still over the Door of the Refectory two very ancient Busts: The one of the glorious *Alfred* the first Founder, the other of *John Erigena*, a *Scotsman*, who first read Lectures there in the Year 882.

The Refectory itself is neat and convenient, adorned

ed with the Pictures of the principal Benefactors, and very good Paintings on Glass of the two Founders. It stands on the South Side of the first Quadrangle. In the Center of which is a Statue of *Cain* and *Abel*.

Through a Passage on the Left-hand of the Gate of the first Quadrangle we enter the second. This is a more modern Structure, and is supposed to have fallen from the Hands of that great Architect Sir *Christopher Wren*.

A Cloister with a Library over it forms the East Side, the Chapel the South. The Area is disposed in the Form of a Garden planted with flowering Shrubs.

The Library is rather calculated for real Use, than ornamental Shew. The Chapel has a Neatness and Simplicity becoming the House of God. If these may be considered as the Parents of Beauty, this Edifice has very strong Pretensions to it. The Roof and Altar-Piece, and East Window, are each respectively fine.

The Ante-Chapel has an elegant Monument to the Memory of the late Principal Dr. *Shippen*, who during his presiding over the College had the utmost Regard to its Interest. His Bust gives the strongest Features of his Face.

The Foundation of this College is for a Principal, twenty Fellows, thirty-two Scholars, and four Exhibitioners.

The Number of Names in the Book at present are about ninety.

Visitor. The Bishop of *Lincoln*.

✝↓✝↓✝↓✝↓✝↓✝↓✝↓✝↓✝↓✝↓✝↓✝↓✝↓✝↓✝↓✝↓✝↓✝↓

HERTFORD College—

——IS situated opposite to the Gate of the Public Schools, consisting of one Court, which about fifty Years ago was begun to be rebuilt. The College

NEW COLLEGE, FROM THE EAST.

lege is intended to be erected in the Form of a Quadrangle, to confift of four Angles, and four intermediate Buildings; each Angle to confift of three Stair-cafes and fifteen fingle Apartments; every Apartment to contain an outward Room, a Bed-place, and a Study. Of thefe the South Eaft Angle, and the Chapel in the South, the Principal's Lodgings in the Eaft, the Hall in the North, and the Gateway (with the Library over it) in the Weft, are already finifhed, agreeable to the Plan of the *Oxford* Almanack of the Year 1747.

Hertford or *Hart-Hall*, an ancient Houfe of Learning, was an Appendant to *Exeter* College. But having received an Endowment in Part, was, at the Requeft of Dr. *Richard Newton*, then Principal, who endowed the Senior Fellowfhips, incorporated, *Sept.* 8, 1740.

And, though it is now ftiled *Hertford* College, it may be called by the Name of any other Perfon who will complete the endowment of it, or become the Principal Benefactor to it.

This College confifts of a Principal, two fenior Fellows or Tutors, Junior Fellows or Affiftants, thirty Undergraduate-Students, and four Scholars.

Vifitor. The Chancellor of the Univerfity.

NEW COLLEGE.

NEW College is fituated Eaft of the *Schools* and Theatre, and North of *Queen's*, from which it is feparated only by a narrow Lane. It is dedicated to St. *Mary Winton*, and has been called *New College* from its firft Foundation, being at that Time highly regarded for its Extent and Grandeur.

We enter this College by a Portal, leading into the firft Court, which is a Quadrangle of about 168 Feet long,

long, and 129 broad, with a Statue of *Minerva* in the Middle of it. This Court, built at the Foundation of the College, was low, with narrow arch'd tranfom Windows, in the Fafhion of the Times: But foon after the Reftoration of King *Charles* II. another Story was added over the old Building, and all the Windows altered to their prefent Form. On the North Side is the Chapel and the Hall; on the Eaft the Library; on the South the Fellows Apartments, and on the Weft the Warden's Lodgings, which are large and commodious, furnifhed with fome valuable Portraits.

· In the North-weft Corner of the Court is the Entrance into the Chapel; by much the grandeft in the Univerfity. The Form of it is like that at *Magdalen* College, but larger. The Ante-Chapel is fupported by two beautiful Staff-moulded Pillars. The large Weftern Window was lately painted by Mr. *Pecket* of *York*. This Part is upwards of 80 Feet long, and 36 broad. The inner Chapel 100 Feet long, 35 broad, and 65 high. As we enter the inner Chapel the moft ftriking Object is the Altar-piece; the Painting whereof was done by our ingenious Countryman Mr. *Henry Cook*, who flourifhed about an hundred Years ago. It reprefents the Concave of a *Semi-Rotunda* in the *Ionic* Order, with a Cupola adorned with curious Mofaic Work; in which, the Eaft End of the Chapel feems to terminate. The Altar, which is partly built of Wood and partly Painted, intercepting in fome Degree the View, greatly favours the *De eptio*; particularly two large open Pannels in the lower Part thereof, which have a good Effect.

In the upper Part of the Altar-piece, which is painted in fuch a Manner as to feem the Finifhing of the Wood-work that fupports it, is a Frame and Pannel, wherein is reprefented the Salutation of the Virgin *Mary*; and above the Entablature hangs hovering a moft beautiful Cloud with great Numbers of Angels and Cherubs in various Attitudes, waiting the Return of the Angel *Gabriel*. The proper Place to view it from to Advantage, is the Entrance into the Choir; the Perspective being contrived on Purpose, to answer that Height and Distance. Over the Communion Table is an Original Painting of the celebrated *Annibal Caracci*, presented to this College by the Earl of *Radnor*. The Subject of this Piece is the Shepherds coming to Christ immediately after his Nativity. The Virgin, Angels, and Shepherds, are represented as jointly celebrating the Nativity in the divine Hymn of " *Glory to God in the Highest, &c.*" The Composition and Drawing is admirable. The Force and Spirit of the Shepherds is finely contrasted by the Elegance and Grace of the Virgin and attending Angels.

The Windows on the South Side are most attracting to Strangers: Each Window containing eight Figures as big as the Life, of Saints and Martyrs, done by Mr. *Price* of *London* in 1737, as those on the North were executed by Mr. *Pecket* of *York* in 1774.

On the North Side of the Chapel is preserved the Crosier of the Founder, which is usually shewn to Strangers; a well-preserved Piece of Antiquity, and almost the only one in the Kingdom. It is near seven Feet high, is of Silver gilt, finely embellished with Variety of rich Gothic Architecture. Though it is about 400 Years old, it has lost little of it's original Beauty.

Here is an admirable Organ, first built by *Dalham*, and since improved by Mr. *Green*, who added to the Clarion Stop, and the Swelling Organ. Cathedral Service is performed here twice every Day, *viz.* at Eight and Five. This Chapel is esteemed one of the best in *England* for Music: which probably is owing to its being very spacious, and having no Breaks (such as Arches and Side Iles) to divide the Sounds. Adjoining to the Chapel is a spacious Cloister, and Garden; on the North Side of which is a Tower with a Peal of Ten Bells.

The Way up to the Hall is at the North-eaſt Corner of the Quadrangle. It is handſomely wainſcotted, and adorned with the Portraits of the Founder *William of Wykeham*, *William* of *Wainfleet* the Founder of *Magdalen* College, and Archbiſhop *Chichele* the Founder of *All-Souls*, both Fellows of this College in the Founder's Life-time.

The LIBRARY (ſituated on the Eaſt Side of the Quadrangle) conſiſts of two elegant Rooms, one over the other, 70 Feet long and 22 broad; both of them well furniſhed with Books, particularly ſome valuable Manuſcripts.

From hence we paſs through the middle Gate into the GARDEN-COURT, which widens by Breaks as we approach the Garden. This Court is ſeparated from the Garden, by an Iron Gate and Palliſade which extend 130 Feet in Length, and admit of an agreeable Proſpect of the Garden through them. In the Garden is a beautiful Mount well diſpoſed, behind which and on the North Side are ſome curious and uncommon Shrubs and Trees. The whole is ſurrounded by a Terras. Great Part of the Garden, as well as ſome Parts of the College, is encompaſſed by the City Wall, which ſerves as a Fence to the College, and is to be traced with its Battlements and Baſtions along the North and South Boundaries of the College.

At the South-eaſt Corner of the Garden we enter the BOWLING-GREEN; which is neat and commodious. Oppoſite to the Entrance is a *Pavilion*; on the Right Flowering Shrubs, and a Row of Elms to ſhade the Green, and on the Left a Row of Sycamores, which are a great Curioſity, nearly incorporated from one End of the Row to the other.

Having conducted our Reader to the furtheſt Part of the College, we would recommend a View of the Building from the Mount; whence the Garden Court, in particular, has a very grand Effect: For from thence

the

the Wings appear properly display'd, and the whole is seen at a convenient Distance. The Perspective View annexed was taken from thence.

The last Curiosity we shall mention, is a beautiful elliptic Arch which is turned over a Lane, for the Conveniency of the Warden to pass into his Garden without coming out at the College Gate. The Lane it is thrown over is without the College, and does not turn at Right-Angles from that leading to the College, but runs obliquely; which renders the Contrivance of it the more artful. A curious Observer will, nevertheless, if he examines the Ribs of the Arch, discover that they form straight Lines from the Abutments on one Side to those on the other, notwithstanding the Whole in a Front-view seems a-twist.

This College was founded by *William Longe*, a Native of *Wykeham* in *Hampshire*, from whence he obtained the Name of *William* of WYKEHAM. His extraordinary Integrity recommended him to the highest Trust and Favours of King *Edward* the Third. When young he was employed by that King in most of the Buildings at that Time carried on by the Crown, particularly in the rebuilding *Windsor* Castle in the magnificent Form in which it now appears. He was soon advanced to some of the most considerable Preferments in the Church, and in 1366 was consecrated Bishop of *Winchester*, in the 43d Year of his Age. His Advancement in the State kept Pace with his Preferment in the Church. In 1364 the King granted him 20.s. per Day out of the Exchequer. He was made Keeper of the Privy Seal in 1364; and Chancellor of *England*, Sept. 17, 1367. *Froissart* says of *Wykeham*, that he was so much in Favour with King *Edward* III. *that every thing was done by him, and nothing was done without him*. His Munificence proceeded always from a constant generous Principle, a true spirit of Liberality. It was not owing to

a casual

a casual Impulse, or a sudden Emotion, but was the Effect of mature Deliberation and prudent Choice.

The Foundation Stone was laid *March* 5th, 1379, and it was finished on *April* 14, 1386, when the Warden and Fellows took Possession of it. In the Year following, St. *Mary's* College near *Winchester* was begun, and was finished and inhabited in the Year 1393, by a Warden, ten Fellows, three Chaplains, three Clerks, and sixteen Choristers; as also two Masters, and seventy Boys, out of whom a certain Number were to be annually elected as a Supply to *New College*. Both which Colleges this pious and munificent Founder saw compleated, making ample Provision for the Support of each, and giving them so regular and perfect a Body of Statutes, that many succeeding Founders have compiled from them. And having survived many Years, he enlarged his Will with costly Legacies of Jewels, Plate, Money, and Books, to be distributed throughout the several Dioceses in which he was preferred, or had temporal Possessions, at his Decease. He died *Sept.* 27, 1404, when he was 80 Years of Age.

The University Sermon is preached here every *Lady-Day* and *Trinity-Sunday* in the Ante-Chapel. Another Custom is the peculiar Manner of calling the Fellows to Dinner and Supper, namely, by a Chorister's going from the Chapel Door to the Garden Gate at One and Seven, crying *à Manger tous Seigneurs*, i. e. *To Dinner or Supper, Gentlemen all*.

The present Members are the Warden, seventy Fellows, ten Chaplains, three Clerks, one Sexton, sixteen Choristers; together with several Gentlemen Commoners.

Visitor. The Bishop of *Winchester*.

WADHAM

WADHAM COLLEGE.

THIS College is situated North of the Public Schools and Printing-House, its Front facing the Gardens of *Trinity* College. It consists chiefly of one large Quadrangle, about 130 Feet square.

The Portico, which leads to the Hall, is adorned with the Statues of King *James* I. and *Nicholas* and *Dorothy Wadham* the Founders. The Buildings of this College have not undergone any Alteration since the Time of the Foundation; and, being built after almost all the others, it has a Regularity and Uniformity above the rest.

The Hall is a spacious Gothic Room at the South-east Angle of the Great Court; and the Library stands on the East of the Hall.

The Chapel is a spacious Edifice, at the North-east Angle of the same great Court, and has that venerable Appearance so remarkable in the Chapels at *New-College* and *Magdalen*, having the Ante-Chapel at right Angles with the Choir. What is most admired here is a very large Window, at the East End, of the Passion of our Saviour, by *Van Ling*, wherein are a great Variety of Figures admirably done, which cost 1500 *l*. The Windows on the Sides seem to be of the same Workmanship; but the greatest Curiosity in this Chapel is the Painted Cloth, if it may be so called, at the lower Part of the Altar. It is the only Work of its Kind at present in *Oxford*; but the Altar-piece of *Magdalen* College, before the new Wainscoting of it, was done in the same Manner. The Cloth itself, which is of an Ash Colour, is the Medium; the Lines and Shades are done with a brown Crayon, and the Lights with a white one: which being afterwards pressed with hot Irons, causing the Damp of the Cloth to incorporate with the Colours, has so fixed them, as to be rendered Proof against a Brush when used to cleanse it from Dust: It was performed by *Isaac Fuller*, who painted the Altar-piece at *Magdalen* College, and it is generally allowed to be masterly Drawing. The East represents the *Lord's Supper*; the North *Abraham* and *Melchisedech*; and the South the *Children of Israel gathering Manna*.

This College was designed by *Nicholas Wadham*, Esq; and built, in Pursuance of his Will, by *Dorothy* his Widow, *Anno* 1613, who appointed a Warden, 15 Fellows, 15 Scholars, two Chaplains, and two Clerks; the Warden to be a Native of *Great Britain*, but to quit the College on his Marriage, or Advancement to a Bishopric. The Fellows, after having completed Eighteen Years from their Regency, to resign their Fellowships. The Scholars, out of whom the Fellows are to be chosen, to be taken three out of *Somersetshire*, and three out of *Essex*; the rest out of any County in *Great Britain*.

The most considerable Benefactor, since the Founder, was *John Goodridge*, M. A. sometime Fellow of this College, who gave all his Estate at *Walthamstowe* in *Essex*, to this Society. Dr. *Hoddy* added ten Exhibitions, four for Students in *Hebrew*, and six for *Greek*, 10 *l.* a Year to each. Lord *Wyndham* 2000 *l.* of which 1500 *l.* to increase the Warden's Salary, and 500 *l.* to beautify and repair the College. Bishop *Lisle*, the late Warden, gave two Exhibitions of 10 *l. per Ann.* each.

The present Members of this Society are the Warden, 15 Fellows, 2 Chaplains, 15 Scholars, two Clerks, and 16 Exhibitioners; the whole Number of Students being usually about 80.

Visitor. The Bishop of *Bath* and *Wells*.

TRINITY

TRINITY COLLEGE.

THE Avenue to *Trinity* College is fenced from the Street by an Iron Pallisade, with folding Gates, opposite the *Turl*. The Front of the College consists of the Chapel and Gateway, with its beautiful Tower.

In the first Court are the Chapel, Hall, and Library.

The great Elegance of the Chapel results from an Assemblage of high finished Ornaments. The Carvings of the Screen and Altar-piece, which are of Cedar, are very Masterly. The exquisite Festoons at the Altar shew the Masterly Hand of that eminent Artist Mr. *Gibbons*. In the midst of the Cieling, which is covered with a beautiful Stucco, is an *Ascension*, which is executed in good Taste, by *Peter Berchett*, an eminent *French* Painter.

The Hall is spacious and well-proportioned, and adorned with Portraits of the Founder and his Lady; and of three Presidents of the College, viz. Drs. *Kettel*, *Bathurst*, and *Sykes*.

In the Library is shewn a valuable Manuscript of *Euclid*; being a Translation from the *Arabic* into *Latin*, before the Discovery of the original *Greek*. It is extremely fair, and contains all the Books. It was given by the Founder, together with several other Manuscripts; who likewise furnished this Library with many costly Volumes, at that Time esteemed no mean Collection.

In the Library Windows are several Compartments of fine old Painted Glass, much injured in former Times. The Painted Glass in the original Chapel of this College, which is reported to have been remarkably beautiful, was entirely destroyed by that Spirit of sacrilegious Zeal so wantonly exercised by the Sons of Fanaticism in the Time of the Usurpation.

The

The second Court is elegant, planned by Sir *Christopher Wren*, and was one of the first Pieces of modern Architecture that appeared in the University. It consists of three Sides, the North and West of which are intended to be raised and finished in the manner with that on the South. The Opening to the Gardens, on the East, has an agreeable Effect.

The Gardens are extensive, and laid out in two Divisions. The first, or larger Division, is chiefly thrown into open Grass-plots. The North Wall is covered with a beautiful Yew Hedge. The center Walk is terminated by a well-wrought Iron Gate, with the Founder's Arms at the Top, supported by two Piers. The Southern Division is a pleasing Solitude, consisting of shady Walks; with a Wilderness of flowering Shrubs, and disposed into serpentine Paths.

This College was founded *March* 8, 1554, by Sir *Thomas Pope*, Knight, of *Tittenbanger*, in *Hertfordshire*, Privy-Councellor to Queen *Mary*, and a singular Friend of Sir *Thomas More*, for the Maintenance and Education of a President, twelve Fellows, and twelve Scholars. The Founder directs, that the Scholars, who succeed to the Fellowships, shall be chosen from his Manors: But if no Candidates appear under such Qualifications on the Day of Election, that they shall be supplied from any County in *England*. He also appoints that no more than two Natives of the same County shall be Fellows of his College at the same Time, *Oxfordshire* excepted, from which County five are permitted.

The principal, and almost only Benefactor, is Dr. *Ralph Bathurst*, formerly President; who expended 1900 *l*. in rebuilding the Chapel.

This College consists of a President, 12 Fellows, and 12 Scholars. These, with the other Members, Gentlemen Commoners, Commoners, &c. amount to near 70.

Visitor. The Bishop of *Winchester*.

BALLIOL

BALLIOL College.

BALLIOL College is situated a little to the Westward of *Trinity*, and consists chiefly of one Court, which we enter by a handsome Gate with a Tower over it. The Buildings about this Court are ancient, except the East End, which is finished in the Manner in which the rest of that Quadrangle is intended to be built.

The Chapel stands at the North-east Angle of the great Court. The great East Window, which is well executed, represents the Passion, Resurrection, and Ascension of Christ. The Hall is at the West End of the same Court. The Master's Lodgings is a convenient Apartment, and has some good Rooms in it, particularly a spacious Hall, having a well preserved ancient Window to the East. Their Library is well furnished with a very large Collection of useful Books, and many ancient Manuscripts.

Over the Gate of the College are the Arms of the *Balliol* Family.

And on the Outside, over against the Master's Lodgings, was a Stone placed Edge-ways, in Memory of those learned and pious Prelates, Archbishop *Cranmer*, Bishop *Ridley*, and Bishop *Latimer*, who were burnt at that Place for their Adherence to the Reformation.

Besides this Court, there is an Area to the North-west, consisting of several detached Lodgings for the Students; and an elegant new Building, rather resembling a modern Dwelling-house, with a beautiful Front to the Street, erected at the Expense of Mr. *Fisher*, in which are several handsome Apartments. This Inscription is on the North Side, by Desire of the Founder:
VERBUM NON AMPLIUS FISHER.

Sir *John Balliol*, of *Bernard* Castle in *Yorkshire*, Father of *John Balliol*, King of *Scotland*, first designed the Foundation of this College for the Education of Scholars, to whom he gave yearly Exhibitions till he could provide them an House; but dying before he purchased one, he recommended the Design to his Widow *Devorguilla*, Daughter of *Alexander* III. King of *Scotland*, who first settled these Exhibitions; and in 1263 purchased a Tenement for her *Scholars of Balliol*, and conveyed it to the Master and Scholars of this House for ever for their Habitation, having obtained a Royal Charter for that Purpose. She afterwards added several new Buildings to it, and settled Lands for the Maintenance of the Scholars, dedicating her Foundation to the Honour of the Holy Trinity, the Blessed Virgin, and St. *Katherine* the Martyr: which Benefactions were afterwards ratified by her Son *John Balliol*, King of *Scotland*, and *Oliver* Bishop of *Lincoln*, in whose Diocese *Oxford* then was. The Value of the Lands and Revenues, belonging to this College, did not exceed 27 *l*. 9 *s*. 4 *d*. per *Ann*. at that Time; but their Estates were soon after greatly enlarged by the Benefactions of others, particularly Sir *Philip Somerville*, a Gentleman in *Staffordshire*, granted to this College the Impropriation of the Parish of *Mickle-Benton* in the County of *Northumberland*; Sir *William Felton*, another Benefactor; and Dr. *John Warner*, Bishop of *Rochester*, founded four *Scotish* Exhibitions, endowing them with an ample Revenue.

John Snell, Esq; gave the Manor of *Ufton* in *Warwickshire* for the Use of *Scots* Exhibitioners.

The Members of this Society are at present a Master, twelve Fellows, fourteen Scholars, and eighteen Exhibitioners: the whole Number of Students amounting to about 50.

The Master and Fellows elect their Visitor, who at present is the Archbishop of *Canterbury*.

St.

St. JOHN's College—

IS situated North of *Balliol* and *Trinity* Colleges, having a Tetras, with a Row of lofty Elms before it.

The Buildings of this College chiefly consist of two large Quadrangles. We enter the first by a handsome old Gateway with a Tower over it. It is formed by the Hall and Chapel on the North, the President's Lodgings on the East, and the Chambers of the Fellows, Scholars, and other Students, on the South and West Sides. The Hall is elegant, being well proportioned, and handsomely wainscotted, with a beautiful arch'd Roof, a Screen of Portland Stone, and a grand variegated Marble Chimney-piece, containing a Picture of St. *John* the Baptist, by *Titian*. It is likewise adorned with many other Pictures; *viz.* at the upper End, by a whole-length Portrait of the Founder; on his Right-hand Archbishop *Laud*, and on his Left Archbishop *Juxon*. On the North and South Sides of the Room are those of Bishop *Mew*, Bishop *Buckridge*, Sir *William Paddy*, and other eminent Men who have been Members of, and Benefactors to, this Society.

North of the Hall is the Common Room, handsomely wainscotted, with a Chimney-piece of Dove-coloured Marble, and a Cieling curiously adorned with Compartments and Shell-work in Stucco, by Mr. *Roberts*.

The Chapel, which is adjoining to the Hall, is in all Respects neat and commodious. It is divided from the Ante-Chapel by a new elegant Screen, over which has lately been erected a very complete new Organ built by Mr. *Byfield*. It has now an Elegance which results from several high-finished yet simple Ornaments.

In particular the Stand on which the Bible is placed is adorned with Masterly Carving. The Altar is of the Corinthian Order, and very properly adapted. Over the Communion Table is a fine Piece of Tapestry, representing our Saviour with the two Disciples at *Emmaus*, copied from a Painting of *Titian*. The Dog snarling at the Cat under the Table, cannot be overlook'd. Nor will the curious Observer be at much Loss, by the striking Likenesses in the four Figures, in discovering they are the then Pope, Kings of *France* and *Spain*, and *Titian*, in the Characters of our Saviour, his Disciples, and Servant. On the North Side of the Choir, in a Marble Urn, is the Heart of Dr. *Richard Rawlinson*. In this Chapel is performed Cathedral Service twice a Day, at Eleven and Five.

Through a Passage on the East Side of the first Quadrangle we enter the second; on the East and West Sides whereof are handsome *Piazzas* in the *Grecian* Taste, each Column consisting of one single bluish Stone, dug from a Part of the College Estate near *Fifield* in *Berkshire*. In the Center of each *Piazza* is a magnificent Gateway, consisting principally of two Orders, 1. The *Doric*, which forms the Gateway itself, agreeable to that of the *Piazzas*. 2. The *Ionic*, which supports a semicircular Pediment. Between four of these Columns, *viz*. two on each Side, in a Niche, is a Brass Statue; that on the East of King *Charles* I. and that on the West of his Queen, cast by *Fanelli* of *Florence*. That neither of the *Greek* Orders might be wanting, the 3d, *viz*. the *Corinthian*, is very artfully introduced in the Construction of the Niche. The whole is richly embellished, and is the Design of that celebrated Architect *Inigo Jones*.

The Library includes the upper Story of the South and East Sides. The South Side is well stored with printed Books in all Faculties, regularly disposed. The second with a most valuable Collection of Manuscripts;

in

in which the Book-cases adhering to the Sides, form a spacious Gallery. Here are some valuable Curiosities, the Picture of King *Charles* I, which has the whole Book of Psalms written in the Lines of the Face and on the Hair of the Head. A very beautiful and singular Picture of St. *John* stain'd in Marble. Some curious Missals. A Chinese Dictionary; and several other Curiosities.

The Gardens belonging to this College are extremely agreeable, very extensive, and laid out, with all those Graces which arise from a succession of Beauties so disposed as to strike us gradually and unexpectedly.

This College was founded by Sir *Thomas White*, Alderman and Merchant-Taylor of *London*; and afterwards *Anno* 1557, he endowed it with several considerable Manors, and at his Death bequeathed the Sum of 3000 *l.* to purchase Lands to increase the Revenues of it. He originally designed *Merchant-Taylors* School in *London* for the only Seminary for this College; but being of a more Public Spirit than to confine himself to any one Place, he allowed two Fellowships to the City of *Coventry*, two to *Bristol*, two also to the Town of *Reading*, and one to *Tunbridge*.

The most considerable Benefactors since, have been Sir *William Paddy*, who founded and endowed the Choir, and built that Side of the New Quadrangle, of which the Library is a Part. Archbishop *Laud*, who at the Expense of above 5000 *l.* (exclusive of 400 *l.* for the Statues of the King and Queen, and 200 Ton of Timber which he obtained by Warrant from *Shotover Forest* and *Stow* Wood) added the other three Sides. Archbishop *Juxon*, who gave 7000 *l.* to this College; Dr. *Gibbons*, who bequeathed the perpetual Advowson of the Living of *Paynton* in *Yorkshire*, and 1000 *l.* to buy Books; Dr. *Holmes*, the late worthy President, with his Lady, who gave 15000 *l.* to augment the Salaries of the Officers, and other Uses; and Dr. *Rawlinson*, who
bequeathed

bequeathed a confiderable Number of Books, and the Reverfion of an Eftate in Fee-farm Rents.

The prefent Members are a Prefident, fifty Fellows, two Chaplains, an Organift, five Singing-men, fix Chorifters, and two Sextons. The Number of Students of all Sorts being ufually about feventy.

Vifitor. The Bifhop of *Winchefter*.

WORCESTER College.

Worcefter College is pleafantly fituated on an Eminence, juft above the River *Ifis* and the Meadows, at the Extremity of the Weftern Suburb. At entering into the College, we have the Chapel and Hall on each Side, both of which are 29 Feet in Breadth, and 50 in Length: Thefe are juft built. The Library, which is a magnificent *Ionic* Edifice, on the Weft of the Chapel and Hall, is 100 Feet in Length, fupported by a fpacious Cloifter. It is furnifhed with a fine Collection of Books, chiefly the Library of Dr. *Clarke*, late Fellow of *All-Souls* College; in which is *Inigo Jones*'s Palladio, with his own Manufcript Notes. According to the Plan propofed, this College is to confift of a fpacious Building. The Chambers of the Fellows and Scholars on the North and South, and the Gardens, which are to lie on a Defcent to the River, on the Weft. The Apartment of the Provoft is at the North-weft Angle. From whence this College will enjoy not only the pleafanteft Situation, but be one of the moft elegant Structures in the Univerfity.

The College was founded *Anno* 1714, by Sir *Thomas Cookes*, for a Provoft, fix Fellows, and fix Scholars.

Dr. *Finney* farther endowed it with two Fellowfhips and two Scholarfhips for Students from *Staffordfhire*. Dr. *Clarke* founded fix fellowfhips and three Scholarfhips ships, with a Preference to Clergymen's Sons. And Mrs. *Eaton*, Daughter to Dr. *Eaton*, Principal of *Glocester* Hall founded six Fellowships. Lady *Holford* gave two Exhibitions of 20 *l.* a Year each, for Charter-house Scholars, to be enjoyed Eight Years.

This House was formerly called *Glocester* College, being a Seminary for educating the Novices of *Glocester* Monastery. It was founded A. D. 1283, by *John Giffard*, Baron of *Brimsfield*. When suppressed, at the Reformation, it was converted into a Palace for the Bishop of *Oxford*; but was soon afterwards erected into an Academical Hall, by Sir *Thomas White*, the Founder of St. *John's* College; in which State it continued, 'till it received a Charter of Incorporation and an Endowment from Sir *Thomas Cookes*.

Here are a Provost, twenty Fellows, eleven Scholars, &c. The whole Number about forty.

Visitor. The Chancellor of the University.

EXETER COLLEGE.

THIS College is situated opposite *Jesus* College, the Front whereof is 220 Feet long, in the Center of which is a magnificent Gate and Tower over it. The Composition of each Front (*viz.* that towards the Street and that towards the Quadrangle) is a *Rustic Basement* which forms the Gateway; a *Plinth* whereupon are placed four *Pilasters* of the *Ionic* Order, supporting a semicircular *Pediment*, in the Area of which are the Founder's Arms on a Shield adorned with Festoons; finishing with a *Balustrade* above all. This, with the beautiful arch'd Roof of the Gateway, is justly esteemed an elegant Piece of Workmanship. The Building within chiefly consists of a large Quadrangle, formed by the Hall, the Chapel, the Rector's Lodgings,

ings, and the Chambers of the Fellows and Scholars, and is regular and uniform.

The Gardens are neatly difpofed, and though within the Town, have an airy and pleafant Opening to the Eaft; with a Terras, from whence we have a View of fome of the fineft Buildings in the Univerfity.

The Library is well furnifhed with Books in the feveral Arts and Sciences; and a very valuable Collection of Claffics, given by *Edward Richards*, Efquire.

Sir *John Acland* built the Hall in 1681, and Dr. *Hakewell*, firft Fellow and afterwards Rector, founded the Chapel in the Year 1624.

Walter Stapledon, Bifhop of *Exeter*, Lord Treafurer of *England*, and Secretary of State to King *Edward* II. 1316, obtained a Charter for founding a College where *Hertford* College now ftands; but wanting Room for the Buildings he defigned, he removed his Scholars to the prefent Houfe, and gave it the Name of *Stapledon-Hall*, after his own Name. He founded a Society confifting of Thirteen, *i. e.* A Rector and twelve Fellows; one of whom, the Chaplain, to be appointed by the Dean and Chapter of *Exeter*; eight to be elected out of the Archdeaconries of *Exeter*, *Toinefs*, and *Barnftaple* in *Devonfhire*, and four of the Archdeaconry of *Cornwall*.

Among the fubfequent Benefactors was *Edmund Stafford*, Bifhop of *Exeter*, who obtained Leave to alter the Name of this Houfe, and fettled two Fellowfhips for the Diocefe of *Sarum*. Sir *William Petre* in Queen *Elizabeth*'s Time obtained a new Charter and Statutes, founded eight Fellowfhips for fuch Counties wherever he then had, or his Heirs at any Time after fhould have Eftates; which by this Time comprehends moft of the Counties in *England*. King *Charles* I. added one Fellowfhip for the Iflands of *Jerfey* and *Guernfey*. And by Mrs. *Shiers*'s Benefaction, as completed and fettled by Dr. *Hugh Shortridge*, two other Fellowfhips were

were added, confined to the Counties of *Hertford* and *Surrey*; besides considerable Augmentations to the Revenues of the Society. The last Benefactor was the learned Mr. *Joseph Sanford*, of *Balliol* College, who gave to this Society his very valuable Library.

The present Members are a Rector, 25 Fellows, one Scholar, who is Bible Clerk, two Exhibitioners: The whole Number of Members about eighty.

Visitor. The Bishop of *Exeter*.

JESUS COLLEGE.

THE Front of this College is newly beautified and improved by a very handsome *Rustic Gateway*, and other Additions.

In the first Court the Chapel on the North Side, and Hall on the West, are neat well-proportioned Rooms, the latter having within these few Years been much improved by the Addition of a Cieling and other Ornaments done by Mr. *Roberts*.

The Inner Court, has three Sides uniformly and neatly built (the Hall before-mentioned making the fourth Side of this Quadrangle) and on the West Side of it over the Common Room, &c. is a spacious well furnished Library.

In the Principal's Lodgings is a fine Picture of King *Charles* I. at full Length, by *Vandyke*; and in the Library a half Length of King *Charles* II. and some original Pieces of Dr. *Hugh Price* by *Holben*, Dr. *Mansell*, Sir *Leoline Jenkins*, &c. Benefactors to this College.

Other Curiosities in this College are, 1. a most magnificent Piece of Plate, the Gift of the late Sir *Watkin Williams Wynne*, Bart. for the Use of the Fellows Common Room. And 2. the Statutes of the College written upon Vellum, in the most exquisite Manner, by the

the Reverend Mr. *Parry* of *Shipston upon Stour*, formerly Fellow of this College.

This College was founded by Queen *Elizabeth*, by Charter bearing Date the 27th of *June*, 1571, in the 13th Year of her Reign, for a Principal, eight Fellows, and eight Scholars. The Queen, at the Request of *Hugh Price*, LL. D. a Native of *Brecknock*, and Treasurer of the Church of St. *David's*, granted her Royal Charter of Foundation, and a certain religious House or Cell called *Whiteball*, (which before the Dissolution of Monasteries belonged to the Priory of St. *Fridefwide*) for the Scite of the College, together with such Timber and other Materials as should be wanting for the building of it, out of her Majesty's Forests of *Shotover* and *Stowe*.

The first Endowment of this College was by Dr. *Hugh Price* abovementioned, who, by Deed bearing Date the last Day of the said Month of, *June*, 1571, convey'd to the College by the Stile and Title of *The Principal, Fellows and Scholars of Jesus College, within the City and University of Oxford, of Queen Elizabeth's Foundation*, certain Lands, Messuages and Tenements in the County of *Brecknock*, of the Value of about 160 *l. per Annum*, for the Maintenance and Support of a Principal, eight Fellows, and eight Scholars, being the Number limited in the Original Charter of Foundation; though by Charters since granted at different Times, and the Munificence of subsequent Benefactors, the Number of Fellows and Scholars is now more than doubled.

The principal Benefactors after Dr. *Hugh Price*, who may in some Measure be called the Founder of this originally little Society, were, Sir *Eubule Thelwal*, Kt. Principal of the College, who, besides his Contributions towards the Buildings carried on under his Direction, increased the Number of Fellows from eight to sixteen; Dr. *Francis Mansell*, who was thrice Principal;

cipal; Sir *Leoline Jenkins*; King *Charles* I. Dr. *Griffith Lloyd*, and many others.

As there were two Fellowships and two Scholarships founded in Consequence of Sir *Leoline Jenkins*'s Will, (one of which Fellowships he directed to be called the Fellowship of King *Charles* II. and the other the Fellowship of King *James* II. in grateful Remembrance of the Favours he had received under those two Princes, which enabled him to become a Benefactor to his College and Country;) and one other Fellowship in Pursuance of a Decree in Chancery, directing the Application of the Remainder of his Personal Estate. The Society now consists of a Principal, 19 Fellows and 18 Scholars, besides a considerable Number of Exhibitioners.

Visitor. The Earl of *Pembroke*.

LINCOLN COLLEGE.

IS situated between *All-Saints* Church and *Exeter* College. It consists of two Courts. The first, which we enter under a Tower, is formed by the Rector's Lodgings on the South-East Angle, the Library and Common Room on the North, and Refectory on the East, the Sides of which are 80 Feet each. The Inner or South Court has also a Gate into the Street; and is a Square likewise, but less than the other, being 70 Feet each Way.

The Hall is a handsome Edifice about 40 Feet long, 25 broad, and of a proportionable Height. It was new wainscoted in 1701, chiefly by the Benefaction of the late Lord *Crewe*, Bishop of *Durham*, whose Arms are placed over the Middle of the Screen, as are those of the rest of the Contributors over other Parts of the Wainscot.

The Library is a very neat Room in the North Side

of the Outer Court, over the Common Room. It has been lately new fitted up, fashed and wainscoted at the Expense of Sir *Nathaniel Lloyd*, Knt. sometime Commoner of this College, and afterwards Fellow of *All-Souls*. It is well furnished with Books, and there are in it some antient and valuable Manuscripts.

There is a good Half-length Picture of Bishop *Crewe* at the West End of it, and another of Sir *Nathaniel Lloyd*.

But what is most taken Notice of in this College, is their Chapel, which is situated on the South Side of the Inner Court.

The Screen of it is of Cedar, finely carved, and is mentioned by Dr. *Plott* as a great Curiosity.

The Windows are entirely of Painted Glass, of which there is one large one over the Altar, and four lesser on each Side. In those of the South Side are the Figures of the Twelve Apostles, three in each Window, as large as Life. In the first Window which is is next the Altar, are *Peter, Andrew*, and *James* the Greater: In the 2d, *John, Philip*, and *Bartholomew*: In the 3d, *Matthew, Thomas*, and *James* the Less: In the 4th, *Jude, Simon, and Matthias.*

On the other Side, over against these, are the Figures of twelve of the Prophets. In the First Window, or next to the Altar, are *David, Daniel*, and *Elijah*: In the 2d, *Isaiah, Jeremiah*, and *Ezekiel*: In the 3d, *Amos, Zechariah*, and *Malachi*: In the 4th, *Elisha, Jonah*, and *Obadiah*.

The East Window, which is over the Altar, contains the Types and Anti-types of our Saviour. It is divided into six Partitions: In the first, reckoning from the North, is the Creation of Man in Paradise; and over it the Nativity of our Saviour. In the 2d, the Passing of the *Israelites* through the Red Sea; and over it, our Saviour's Baptism: In the 3d, the Jewish Passover; and over it, the Institution of the Lord's Supper:

per: In the 4th, the Elevation of the Brazen Serpent in the Wilderness; and over it, our Saviour's Crucifixion: In the 5th, *Jonas* delivered out of the Whale's Belly; and over it our Saviour's Resurrection: In the 6th, *Elijah* going to Heaven in the Fiery Chariot; and over it, our Saviour's Ascension.

The Cieling, which is Cedar, is embellished with the Arms of the Founders and the principal Benefactors; intermixed with Cherubims, Palm-branches, Festoons, &c. beautifully painted and gilt. The Lower Cedar Desks are terminated with eight well executed Figures of the same Wood, viz. *Moses* and *Aaron*, the Four Evangelists, St. *Peter* and St. *Paul*.

This Chapel was built in 1630, by Dr. *John Williams*, at that Time Bishop of *Lincoln*, and afterwards Archbishop of *York*; of whom Memorials are to be seen in several Places.

This College was first founded by *Richard Flemming*, who was born of a good Family in *Yorkshire*. He was educated in this University, of which he was two Years Proctor, being then Fellow of *University* College.

In 1420, he was made Bishop of *Lincoln* by King *Henry* V. and died in 1431. He obtained the Charter of Incorporation of King *Henry* VI. in the sixth Year of his Reign; and in 1429 established a College, consisting of a Rector and seven Fellows, to whom he appropriated the Income of the said Churches.

In the Year 1478, *Thomas Scott*, alias *Rotherham*, then Bishop of *Lincoln*, considering the Imperfect State of this Foundation, obtained a new Charter of King *Edward* IV. by Virtue whereof, he added five other Fellowships to the seven before founded, annexed to the College the Rectories of *Long Combe* in *Oxfordshire*, and *Twyford* in *Buckinghamshire*, and gave them a Body of Statutes, in which he limits the Choice of the Fellows to the Dioceses of *Lincoln* and *York*, all except one, whom he would have to be of the Diocese of *Wells*.

But

But the greatest Benefactor to this College was the Right Honourable *Nathaniel* Lord *Crewe*, late Bishop of *Durham*, who being here in the Year 1717, after contributing liberally to the Buildings which were then carrying on at *Christ Church*, *Queen's*, *Worcester*, and *All-Souls* Colleges, and to the finishing of *All-Saints* Church, settled by Way of a Rent Charge free from all Deductions whatsoever, issuing out of his Manors in *Northumberland* and *Durham*, Twelve Exhibitions of 20 *l. per Annum* each, for Commoners of this College, whom he would have to be the Sons of Gentlemen; and made a considerable Augmentation to the annual Stipends of the Rector, Fellows, Scholars, Bible Clerk, and the Chaplains of the four appropriated Churches. And what much enhanced the Merit of his Beneficence was, that his Benefaction took Place immediately; and they all received their respective Shares of it half yearly, for several Years, while their Great Benefactor was living.

A little before the Time of the second Foundation, *Thomas Beckington*, Bishop of *Bath* and *Wells*, left a considerable Sum of Money to this College, to erect an handsome Apartment for the Rector at the South-east Corner of the Quadrangle. Upon several Parts of which Building is a Device cut in Stone, representing a Beacon and Tun, alluding to the said Benefactor's Name of *Bokyntun*.

After which, *Thomas de Rotheram* compleated the Quadrangle, by building up the Remainder of the South Side of it; on the Wall of which are his Arms curiously carved in Stone in several Places.

The Members of this College are usually between fifty and sixty.

Visitor. The Bishop of *Lincoln*.

ORIEL

ORIEL COLLEGE.

ORIEL College is situated between St. *Mary's* Church on the North, *Corpus Christi* College on the South, and *Christ Church* on the West; the Entrance is on the West. It chiefly consists of one regular, uniform, well-built Quadrangle. On the North Side whereof is the Library and the Provost's Lodgings; on the East the Hall, and the Entrance into the Chapel, which runs Eastward from thence; and on the South and West Sides are the Chambers of the of the Fellows and other Students.

Opposite to the Great Gate we ascend by a large Flight of Steps, having a Portico over them, to the Hall; which is a well-proportioned Room, handsomely wainscotted, with a *Doric* Entablature, and adorned with three Whole-length Portraits, *viz.* in the Middle, at the Upper-end a very fine one of King *Edward* II. enthroned with his *Regalia*, by *Hudson*; on his Right Hand, one of Queen *Anne* by *Dahl*; and on his Left, one of the late Duke of *Beaufort*, in his Parliament-robes, having a Negro Servant bearing his Coronet, by *Seldi*.

The Chapel, which has been lately repaired and ornamented, has that Beauty which is derived from a decent Simplicity: The large East Window, *The Wise Men offering*, was lately painted by Mr. *Peckett*, from a Design by Dr. *Wall*.

Through a Passage on the North Side, we enter the Garden Court. The Garden is fenced at this End with a Pair of Iron Gates and Palisades, properly supported by a Dwarf-Wall and Stone Piers. On either Hand is a Wing of new Building, in a Style conformable to the Quadrangle. That on the Right, was built at the Expense of Dr. *Robinson*, Bishop of *London*: And that on the Left by Dr. *Carter*, late Provost; Part thereof being intended as an Addition to the Provost's Lodgings.

This College was founded by King *Edward* II. 1324. King *Edward* III. and *Adam le Brome*, Almoner to King *Edward* III. who was the first Provost, were considerable Benefactors to this College. King *Edward* III. particularly gave them the Large Messuage of *Le Oriel*, situate in St. *John*'s Parish, by which Name the College was afterwards called; from whence this College has been frequently held to be a Royal Foundation: But the first Grant was made to St. *Mary Hall*, from whence the Fellows removed to *Oriel*, after that House was assigned to them. He likewise gave them the Hospital of St. *Bartholomew*, near *Oxford*, with the Lands thereunto belonging.

Other Benefactors were *John Frank*, Master of the Rolls in the Reign of *Henry* VI. who gave 1000*l.* to this College at his Death, to purchase Lands for the Maintenance of four Fellows; *John Carpenter*, formerly Provost, and afterwards Bishop of *Worcester*; *William Smith*, Bishop of *Lincoln*, and Dr. *Richard Dudley*, sometime Fellow, and afterwards Chancellor of the Church of *Sarum*, gave the College the Manor of *Swaynswick* in *Somersetshire*, for the Maintenance of two Fellows and six Exhibitioners. Dr. *John Tolson*, who was Provost in 1640, was the principal Benefactor to the present Edifice, to which Purpose he gave 1150*l.* and other considerable Donations. Queen *Anne* annexed a Prebend of *Rochester* to the Provost for ever. Dr. *Robinson*, Bishop of *London*, besides the New Building, gave 2500*l.* to augment the Fellowships. And the late Duke of *Beaufort* gave 100*l. per Annum* for four Exhibitioners.

The present Members are a Provost, eighteen Fellows, and fourteen Exhibitioners; the whole Number of Students of all Sorts about eighty.

Visitor. The Lord Chancellor.

CORPUS.

CORPUS-CHRISTI COLLEGE.

CORPUS-CHRISTI College ſtands between *Chriſt-Church* on the Weſt, *Merton* College on the Eaſt, and *Oriel* College on the North; conſiſting of one Quadrangle, an elegant Pile of modern Buildings, in which are pleaſant and commodious Rooms (that look into *Merton* and *Chriſt-Church* Meadows) and a Cloiſter adjoining; alſo a neat Structure which looks Eaſtwards towards *Merton* College Grove, in which are Apartments appropriated to Gentlemen-Commoners, whoſe Number the Founder has confined to Six, and who are to be Sons of Noblemen, or other eminent Perſons.

On the Eaſt Side of the Quadrangle is the Hall, which is 50 Feet long, and 25 broad, and of a proportionable Height.

The *Cylindrical* Dial in the Quadrangle is ſet at Right Angles with the *Horizon*, the common Sections whereof, with the Hour Circles, except the *Meridian* Circle that divides it by the *Axis*, as alſo the *Equinoctial*, are all Ellipſes, and is a fine old Piece of *Gnomonicks*. On the Column is a perpetual Kalendar.

The Chapel, which is ſituated at the South-eaſt Corner of the Quadrangle, is 70 Feet in Length, and 25 in Breadth.

The Library is well furniſhed with Books, particularly a large Collection of Pamphlets from the Reformation to the Revolution. About 300 MSS. An *Engliſh* Bible, ſuppoſed to be older than *Wickliffe*'s. A Parchment Roll, containing the Pedigree of the Royal Family, and the ſeveral Branches of it, from King *Alfred* to *Edward* VI. with their Arms blazoned, ſigned by the King at Arms; and ſeveral other Curioſities, particularly an ancient Manuſcript Hiſtory of the Bible in

French;

French, finely decorated with curious Paintings, given by General *Oglethorpe*, who was a Member of this College; and also a very valuable Collection of the first Editions of the Classics.

They shew here also the genuine Crosier of the Founder, a Piece of curious Workmanship, little impaired by Time.

This College was founded in the Year 1516, by Dr. *Richard Fox*, a Native of *Ropesley*, near *Grantham* in *Lincolnshire*, who was successively Bishop of the Sees of *Exeter*, *Bath* and *Wells*, *Durham* and *Winchester*, and was likewise Lord Privy Seal to King *Henry* VII. and *Henry* VIII. He first intended it only as a Seminary for the Monks of the Priory, or Cathedral Church of St. *Swithin* at *Winchester*, and obtained a Charter for that End; but altered his Mind by the Persuasion of *Hugh Oldham*, Bishop of *Exeter*, who engaged to be a Benefactor to the House, on condition that he would convert it into a College for the Use of secular Students, after the Manner of other Colleges in the University: Whereupon Bishop *Fox* caused the first Charter to be cancelled, and obtained another, whereby he was permitted to found a College for the Study of Divinity, Philosophy, and other liberal Arts. The Charter of Foundation was dated at the Castle of *Wolvesly*, on the Calends of *March* 1516.

He assigned a Body of Statutes for the Government of this Society, whereby he appointed, that the Fellows should be elected out of the Scholars, who are to be chosen from the Counties or Dioceses following, *viz.* two *Surry*, three *Hampshire*, one *Durham*, two *Bath* and *Wells*, two *Exeter*, two County of *Lincoln*, two *Gloucestershire*, one *Wiltshire*, or (in Defect of a Candidate) the Diocese of *Sarum*, one County of *Bedford*, two County of *Kent*, one County of *Oxford*, one *Lancashire*.

Among the Benefactors was *Hugh Oldham*, Chaplain to *Margaret* Countess of *Richmond*, and afterwards Bishop

Merton College from the Meadows.

shop of *Exeter*, who gave 6000 Marks towards the building of this College, besides several Estates for the Endowment of it.

William Frost, Steward to the Founder; *John Claymond*, the first President of this College; and *Robert Morwent*, second President, gave to the College several Portions of Lands: And in 1706, Dr. *Turner*, when President, gave the New Buildings, and his Collection of Books.

The present Members of this Society are a President, 20 Fellows, 2 Chaplains, 20 Scholars, 4 Exhibitioners, and 6 Gentlemen-Commoners.

Visitor. The Bishop of *Winchester*.

MERTON COLLEGE.

MERTON College is situated East of *Corpus Christi*, and consists of three Courts. The largest, or inner Court, is about 110 Feet long, and 100 broad.

The Chapel is at the West End of the first Court, and is likewise the Parish Church of St. *John Baptist de Merton*. It is one of the largest and best proportion'd *Gothic* Structures in the University, 100 Feet in Length, and 30 in Breadth, and has a very capacious Tower, and Ante-Chapel. But large as it is at present, it has been thought, from its whole Appearance, and from the Form and Manner of the Arches closed up in the Wall of the West End, on each Hand of the great Window, to have been built with a View to a farther Addition of a Nave and Side-Isles; the present Building being no more than the Choir, and Cross-Isle. Such a Design was more easy to be made than executed, and after all, most likely reached no farther than to the carrying on the Building, as far as it went, in the Cathedral Manner.

In the Chapel are the Monuments of Sir *Thomas Bodley*,

ly, Sir *Henry Saville*, Bishop *Earle*, and some others. In the Ante-Chapel, besides the rest, by the North Door, is that of Mr. *Anthony Wood*, the famous Antiquarian. And near the Entrance into the Chapel is a very neat though small one, for the late Warden Dr. *Wyntle* and his Sister.

The Hall is between the first and the inner Court; and the Library in the small old Quadrangle, South of the Chapel, and is well furnished with ancient and modern Books and Manuscripts.

The Gardens are very pleasant, having the Advantage of a Prospect of the adjacent Walks and Country from the South Terras.

This Society, consisting of a Warden and about the same Number of Scholars or Fellows as at present, was first placed at *Maldon* in *Surry*, (but with a Provision for the Abode and Residence of the chief Part of them here in *Oxford*) Anno 1264, the 48th Year of King *Henry* the Third, by *Walter de Merton*, sometime Lord Chancellor of *England*, and then after Bishop of *Rochester*: The Instrument of Endowment, with the Statutes under the Broad Seal, the Founder's, the Bishop of the Diocese's, and that of his Chapter, being at this Time in the College Treasury, and deemed to be the first Charter of the Kind in *Europe*. Not long after, *viz.* the Year 1267, he gave the Statutes in their present Form, transferring the whole Society from *Maldon* to St. *John Baptist's* Street, in *Oxford*, and placing them in a House or College he had built there. The Statutes then given were superseded for a short Time by an intermediate Charter with others in 1270, but were replaced and finally established under the Broad Seal and his own, *Anno* 1274, the second of the Reign of King *Edward* the First.

Such was the Original of this ancient Society, by these Charters, five hundred Years since, incorporated, and endowed with almost all the Lands they at this

Time

Time possess, and provided with the same Statutes which, without any Alteration or Addition, they are now governed by.

These, by the Recourse had to them, were of much Use to the After-Foundations both here and in *Cambridge*, and indeed to those likewise which have the Precedency [*]. And with so much Prudence was this College founded, that King *Edward* the First recommended it to *Hugh de Balsham*, Bishop of *Ely*, as a Model for his intended Munificence in *Cambridge*, according to which *Peter-House* [†], the first College was afterwards erected in that University. And farther, it is said of the Founder of *Merton* College, that though in reality he was the Founder of only one, by Example he was the Founder of all the other Colleges [‡].

The Post-masters in this House are of a distinct and different Foundation, which took Place about an hundred Years after the other. *John Williot*, S. T. P. who was Chancellor of *Exeter*, and had been Fellow of this College, and Chancellor of the University, giving all his Real, and most of his Personal Estate, for the Support and Education of them. Mr. *John Chamber*, Canon of *Windsor*, and Fellow of *Eton*, and once Fellow of this College, at his Decease in 1604, made Provision for two additional ones to be always sent at the Nomination and Appointment of the Provost of *King's* and *Eton* Colleges from *Eton* School. The Number then became fourteen: And their Revenues have been since

---

[*] *University* and *Balliol*.——Their first and earliest Statutes to be seen in *Smith*'s Annals of *University* College, and in Dr. *Savage*'s *Balliofergus*) were of a later Date, and therefore capable of this Advantage: But some of their successive ones more plainly had it, and Sir *Philip Somervyle*'s in particular, besides the General Form, &c. are in many Places Word for Word the same as those of this College.

[†] The Statutes of *Merton* College are also referred to for their Rule and Direction in the Statutes of *Simon Montacute*, Bishop of *Ely*, who about half a Century after completed this Foundation.

[‡] See the Inscription upon his Monument in *Rochester* Cathedral.

increased

increased by *Thomas Jessop*, M. D. sometime Fellow of the College, and other Benefactors.

Besides the Post-Masters, there are now four other Scholars of the Foundation of Mr. *Henry Jackson*, late of this College, which commenced in 1753.

In the Election of a Warden, the Fellows chuse three Persons whom they present to their Visitor, the Archbishop of *Canterbury*, who appoints one of them.

The present Members are a Warden, twenty-four Scholars, fourteen Post-masters, Mr. *Jackson*'s four Scholars, two Chaplains, and two Clerks; the whole Number of Students of all Sorts, being about eighty.

Visitor. The Archbishop of *Canterbury*.

CHRIST CHURCH.

THIS College merits the particular Observation of Strangers. It consists of four Courts or Squares, *viz.* 1. The great Quadrangle; 2. *Peckwater* Square; 3. *Canterbury* Court; 4. The Chaplain's Court; and some other Buildings.

The stately West Front of the great Quadrangle is a magnificent *Gothic* Building, 382 Feet in Length, terminated at each End with two corresponding Turrets. The great Gate is in the Middle of this Front, and over it a beautiful Tower, enriched with *Gothic* Ornaments, designed by Sir *Christopher Wren*, erected by Dr. *Fell*, and admirably corresponding to the Taste of the rest of the Buildings. In this Tower hangs the great Bell, called *Tom*, on the Sound of which the Scholars of the University are to retire to their respective Colleges. Though the Windows in the Front are not exactly regular, yet such are the Greatness of the Proportions, and the Magnificence of the Whole, that they raise the Admiration of every Spectator, and help him

to form an Idea of the great Mind of Cardinal Wolsey. In this Quadrangle are the Statues of Queen *Anne*, Cardinal *Wolsey*, and Bishop *Fell*; that of the Cardinal, by *Francis Bird*, in the South-east Corner is justly admired as an excellent Piece of Workmanship.

The Great Quadrangle is 264 by 261 Feet in the Clear. The Hall, which takes up more than half the South Side, is considerably elevated above the rest, and the whole finished with a Balluftrade of Stone. The South, East, and Part of the West Sides, with the magnificent Kitchen to the South of the Hall, were erected by the Cardinal.

The East and North Sides of this Quadrangle are taken up with the Dean's and four of the Canons Lodgings.

In the Year 1638, the North Side of the grand Quadrangle was begun. On the Restoration, this Part of Building was refumed, by the Direction and Encouragement of Dr. *Fell*, then Dean of the College; and finished *Anno* 1665.

The Hall is by far the most magnificent Room of the Kind in *Oxford*, and perhaps one of the largest in the Kingdom. The Roof is framed of Timber curiously wrought, and so contrived, as to produce a very grand and noble Effect. There are near 300 Compartments in the Cornice, which are embellished with as many Coats of Arms carved and blazoned in their proper Colours.

At the upper End of the Hall there is an Ascent of three Steps which run through the whole Breadth; near which is a beautiful *Gothic* Window in a Recess, that demands the Attention of the Curious.

This fuperb Room is beautified, and improved, by compleating and painting the Wainfcot and Roof, and the Addition of a great Number of Portraits of former Deans, Bifhops, and other great Men, that were bred at the College, which are difpofed round the Room in the following Manner.

Over

Over the High Table.

Compton, Bishop of London.   Corbet, Bishop of Norwich.

HENRY VIII. a Full Length.

| King, Bp of Lond. | Duppa, Bp of Winton | Cardinal Wolsey. | Fell, Bp of Oxon. | Morley, Bp of Winton. | Boulter, Abp of Armagh. |

An original Head of Henry VIII.

A Bust of His Majesty.

On the South Side, beginning at the upper End.

Wake, Abp of Canterbury.
Potter, Abp of Canterbury.
Smalridge, Bp of Bristol.
Trevor, Bp of Durham.
Lord Mansfield.
Hooper, Bp of Bath and Wells.
Benson, Bp of Gloucester.
Este, Bp of Waterford.
Stone, Abp of Armagh.
Robinson, Abp of Armagh.
Tanner, Bp of St. Asaph.
Morton, Bp of Meath.
Fuller, Bp of Lincoln.
Gastrel, Bp of Chester.
Hickman, Bp of Londonderry.
Sanderson, Bp of Lincoln.
Mr. Alsop.

Over these.

Westfaling, Bp of Hereford.
Peers, Abp of York.
Heton, Bp of Ely.
Pidwson, Bp of Durham.
Godwin, sen. Bishop of Bath and Wells.

Underneath.

Sam. Fell, Dean of Ch. Church.
Griffith Bp of St. Asaph.

On the North Side, beginning at the upper End.

Sir John Dolben, Abp of York.
Sir J. Trelawney, Bp of Winton.
Wood, Bp of Litchfield and Cov.
Drummond, Abp of York.
Blackbourn, Abp of York.
Cox, Abp of Cashel.
Dr. Stratford, Canon of Ch. Ch.
Dr. Friend, M. D.
Welbore Ellis, Esq;
Dr. Aldrich, Dean of Ch. Ch.
Dr. Nicol, Canon of Ch. Ch.
Richard Frewen, M. D.
Sir J. Dolben, Preb. of Durham.
Dr. Friend, Master of Westminster School.
Dr. Busby, Mast. of West. School.
Dr. Sprat, Archdeacon of Rochest.

Over these.

Smith, Bp of Gloucester.
James, Bp of Durham.
Ravis, Bp of London.
Bancroft, Bp of Oxford.
Matthews, Abp of York.
Godwin, jun. Bishop of Landaff.

Underneath.

An Orig. of King, Bp. of London.

Over the Screen, and on each Side, in the following Order.

Lord Arlington.

Ellis, Bp of Kildare.   Lord Mansfield.   Sir Dudley Carelton.

A Bust of GEORGE I. in Marble.

King, Bp of Chichest.   Sir Gilb. Dolben.   Locke.   E. of Orrery.
Peter Martyr, Canon of Ch. Ch.   The

The Church of this College, which is the Cathedral of the Diocese, is on the East of the Grand Quadrangle, a venerable Structure, originally the Church of St. *Fridefwide*'s Monastery. The Roof of the Choir is a beautiful Piece of Stone-work put up by Cardinal *Wolfey*, who also rebuilt the Steeple. The East Window was painted by Mr. *Price*, senior, of *London*, after a Design of Sir *James Thornhill*, representing the *Epiphany*. In the *Dormitory*, which is an Isle on the North Side of the Choir, is the Tomb of St. *Fridefwide*, who died A. D. 739. In the same Place is a Window, curiously painted, representing St. *Peter* delivered out of Prison by the *Angel*: Beside the principal Figures, there are a considerable Number of *Roman* Soldiers in various sleeping Attitudes, admirably well drawn: And, though a very small Portion of the Glass is stained, the Colours are brilliant, and the Whole appears very lively. It was painted by *J. Oliver*, in his Eightieth Year, and given by him to the College in the Year 1700. In this and other Parts of the Church are some Monuments, no less remarkable for their elegant Inscriptions than their beautiful Structure.

In the Tower are ten celebrated Bells, brought from *Ofeney* Abbey, as was the great Bell, called *Tom*, above-mentioned.

In this Church Choir Service is performed every Day at Ten and Five; except on *Sundays* and Holidays, when it is at Eight in the Morning.

Three Sides of *Peckwater* Court are uniform, designed by Dr. *Aldrich*, then Dean, no less famous for his Skill in Architecture, than for his Eminence in most other Branches of Knowlege. Each Side contains 15 Windows in Front. The lower Story is *Rustic*, in which are three Entrances. The second Story, and the *Attic* above it are contained in the Height of the *Ionic* Order, which rests upon the *Rustic*. Over the five Middle Windows in each Side is a beautiful Pediment, which projects,

jects, supported by Three-quarter Columns of the same Order, as the Entablature and Balluftrade of the other Parts are by Pilafters.—On the fourth Side of this Court is a magnificent Library, 141 Feet long, built in the *Corinthian* Order, the Pillars of which are four Feet in Diameter. Underneath was intended a Piazza opening to the Square, with feven Arches, and an Afcent of three Steps running the whole Length of the Building. This Defign has been fince altered, for the more convenient Reception of the great Collection of Books belonging to the College. The Wainfcoting, Book-cafes, and Stucco Work, as well on the Stair-cafe, as in the Rooms of the Library, are very highly finifhed, particularly the beautiful Feftoons in Stucco, charged with fymbolical Imagery, feverally reprefenting the particular Branch of Literature contained beneath. In the lower Apartments, both to the right and left, are depofited the celebrated Collection of Pictures given to the College by General *Guife*; among which are fome from the Collection of King *Charles* I. A Portrait by *Titian*. The Flight into *Egypt* by *Guido Reni*. The Family of the *Caracci*'s, reprefented in a Butcher's Shop, the moft celebrated Performance of *Annibal Caracci*. Two Nativities by *Titian*. *Jefus* and St. *John* embracing by *Raphael*. A Nativity, by *Raphael*. The Fable of *Erichthonius* delivered to the Nymphs to be educated, by *Salvator Rofa*. A *Venus* and *Cupid*, by *Titian*. St. *Francis* in a Vifion, fupported by Angels, by *Annibal Caracci*. An *Ecce Homo*, by *Ludovico Caracci*. A *Medufa*'s Head by *Rubens*. The Pale of an Altar, with Figures larger than the Life, by *Corregio*. Two Half-lengths of Women, by *Domenichino*.

Upon a Pedeftal, in the Recefs on the North Side of the upper Apartment, is an admirable Statue of Mr. *Locke*, formerly Student of this Houfe, by *Roubillac*.

Canterbury Court, formerly *Canterbury* College, is a fmall Court, Eaft of *Peckwater*, confifting of fome of
the

the old Buildings, though good Apartments, on the South Side; a superb arch'd Gateway on the East; and on the East and South, new Buildings for the Students and other Members. The Gateway is the Architecture of the celebrated Mr. *Wyatt*.

The Chaplains Court is situated South-east of the grand Quadrangle, on the North Side whereof is a large Building of new Chambers; the Walls of which was the Hall or Refectory of St. *Fridefwide*'s Priory.

The Court of the Grammar School is South of the great Quadrangle, having the Hall on the North Side of it: Under Part of the Hall is the Common Room, very spacious, in which is a superb Marble Chimney-piece, and over it an excellent Bust, by *Ryfbrac*, of Dr. *Bufby*, formerly Master of *Westminster* School, a considerable Benefactor to the College. Round the Room are the Pictures of several of the Masters of the same School, and other eminent Men belonging to the College. On the South Side is the new Anatomical Theatre, erected and endowed by the late Dr. *Lee*, Physician to King *George* II. at the Expence of 20,000 *l*. with a proper Stipend to the Lecturer, &c. In it is a fine Collection of Anatomical Preparations and Injections. There is also an elegant Range of Buildings, usually called *Fell*'s, looking towards the Gravel Walk. The Gravel Walk, planted on each Side with Elms, deserves our Notice, being a Quarter of a Mile in Length, and of a proportionable Breadth. It commands a pleasant Prospect of the Meadows, the *Thames*, and some adjacent Villages.

This College was founded by Cardinal *Wolfey*, upon the Place where formerly stood the Priory of St. *Fride-fwide*, which, with several other religious Foundations, were dissolved, in order to endow the new College intended by the Cardinal. The Design was far from being compleated at the Time of the Cardinal's Disgrace, little more being built than the East, South, and Part

of

the West Sides of the great Quadrangle, and the Kitchen. And as to the Foundation itself, whatever it might be at that Time, 'tis certain it was afterwards lessened, and the Form of it altered two or three Times by the King. The Disgrace of the Cardinal happened in the Year 1529, when the King seized upon this College, as well as the other Estates belonging to the Cardinal. In the Year 1532, at the Instance of Lord *Cromwell*, the King new-modelled the Foundation, and gave it the Name of *King Henry the Eighth's College*. This was suppressed in 1545, and in the Year following, 1546, the Episcopal See was removed from *Oseney* to this College, and the Church of St. *Frideswide* constituted a Cathedral, by the Name of *Christ's Church*.

This Foundation has continued in the same Form ever since. It consists of a Dean, eight Canons, 101 Students, (four or five of which are elected annually from *Westminster* School, and the other Vacancies as they happen, are filled up by the Canons) 8 Chaplains, 8 Singing-Men, and as many Choristers, a Schoolmaster, an Usher, an Organist, &c. Since the Time of Queen *Elizabeth*, this College has largely experienced the Bounty of several Benefactors, particularly Bishop *Fell*, who left ten Exhibitions of 10 *l. per Ann.* to Commoners, whose good Behaviour for a Year should recommend them to the Favour of the College, and to be held for ten Years from the Time they were nominated to them. The 101st Studentship was added by *William Thurston*, Esq; 1663, and is now in the Gift of the *Vernon* Family. Several Exhibitions of 13 *l. per Ann.* were given by Lady *Holford*, for Scholars educated at the *Charter-House*; and several more by other Benefactors.

Visitor. The King.

PEMBROKE

PEMBROKE COLLEGE.

*P*Embroke College, so called from the Earl of *Pembroke*, Chancellor of the University at the Time it was founded, is situated near St. *Aldate*'s Church, in a direct Line from the grand Gate of *Christ Church*, and consists of two small Courts. The Quadrangle is neat and uniform, having the Hall at the North-west Angle, in which are Pictures of the Founders and some Benefactors. The Chapel is a small, elegant Building, of the *Ionic* Order, with a beautiful Altar-piece. In the Garden, which is West of the Chapel, is a pleasant Common Room, and a Terras-walk. The Master's Lodgings, which join to the College on the North, is a handsome modern Edifice.

This College, formerly *Broadgate* Hall, was founded An. 1620, by *Tho. Tesdale*, of *Glympton*, Esq; and *Richard Whitwick*, S. T. B. Rector of *Ilsley*, *Berks*, for a Master, ten Fellows, and ten Scholars. Four of Mr. *Tesdale*'s Fellows to be chosen out of his Relations, and the rest to come from *Abingdon* Free School.

As to Mr. *Whitwick*'s Benefaction, two of the Fellows and two Scholars to be of his Kindred, and the rest from *Abingdon* School.

King *Charles* I. granted to this Society the perpetual Advowson of St. *Aldate*'s Church; and certain Lands, for the Maintenance of one Fellow, to be chosen from *Guernsey* or *Jersey*.

Archbishop *Abbot*, *Juliana Stafford*, and *Francis Rous*, were the next Benefactors; and Dr. *George Morley*, Bishop of *Winchester*, founded five Scholarships for the Natives of *Guernsey* and *Jersey*.

Queen *Anne* annexed a Prebend of *Gloucester* to the Mastership. Lady *Holford* gave two Exhibitions of 20*l*. a Year each; Dr. *Hall*, Master of this College, and Bishop of *Bristol*, built the Master's Lodgings; Sir *John Bennet*, Lord *Ossulstone*, endowed two Fellowships and Scholarships; Mr. *Townsend* gave eight Exhibitions to young Scholars from *Gloucestershire*; and Sir *John Phillips*, Bart. in 1749, founded one Fellowship and one Scholarship.

The present Members are a Master, fourteen Fellows, 30 Scholars and Exhibitioners; the whole Number of Students usually about 70.

Visitor. The Chancellor of the University.

HALLS.

FIVE Halls or Academical Houses, not incorporated, are still remaining. Originally the Students lived chiefly in these Academical Halls or *Hotels*, where Professors and Tutors resided. But when the Colleges were founded, and still more, when the Reformation took Place, the liberal Education, now in Use, brought most of the Students to the more convenient Accommodation in Colleges. These Societies are not endowed, and are under the Government of their respective Principals, whose Income arises from the Room-rent of the Chambers. The Students take an Oath to obey the Statutes and Customs of the Hall, which Statutes are made and altered by the Chancellor, who has the Nomination of the Principals, and is Visitor of all the Halls, except St. *Edmund* Hall, which is dependant on *Queen*'s College, the Principal of it being appointed by that Society.

ST. ALBAN HALL.

I. ST. ALBAN HALL, which is in St. *John*'s Parish, adjoins to *Merton* College on the East. It was founded by *Robert de St. Alban*, out of Part of the Lands belonging

longing to the Abbey of *Littlemore.* Of this Hall were Archbishop *Marsh*; Dr. *Lamplugh*, Archbishop of *York*; *Benedict Barnham*, Alderman of London, who built the Front of the Hall as it is at present; and *William Lenthall*, Esq; Speaker of the Long Parliament.

ST. EDMUND HALL.

II. ST. EDMUND HALL, is opposite to the East Side of *Queen's*; to which College it is dependant, and has about 25 Students. The Buildings were compleated, and other considerable Improvements made by the late Principal, Dr. *Shaw.* Of this Hall were Dr. *John Mill*, who published the *Greek* Testament, printed at the *Theatre*; and *Thomas Hearne*, M. A. that diligent Antiquarian.

NEW-INN-HALL.

III. NEW-INN-HALL stands at the West End of the City, near the Church of St. *Peter* in the Bailey. It was formerly called *Trillock's-Inn* from *John Trillock*, Bishop of *Hereford*, who founded it in the Year 1349. Opposite this Hall is the Gateway of a College of Monks of the *Augustine* Order, in which *Erasmus* resided two Years. He left an elegant *Latin* Poem on his Manner of Living there.

ST. MARY HALL.

IV. ST. MARY HALL is situated North of *Oriel* College, near the *High-Street.* It consists of one Quadrangle, with a Garden inclosed in the Middle of it. It is formed by the Principal's Lodgings on the North, the Hall and Chapel on the South, and on the East and West by the Chambers of the Students.

This Hall was founded by King *Edward* II. Some Exhibitions have been given to assist the Students in the Prosecution of their Studies.

Several eminent Men have resided here, *viz.* Cardinal *Allen*, Sir *Thomas Moore*, *Erasmus*, Mr. *Sandys* the celebrated *English* Poet and Traveller, *&c.*

MAGDALEN HALL.

V. MAGDALEN HALL is adjoining to the West Side of *Magdalen* College, to which it is an Appendant. The Number of Exhibitions given to this Hall supplies it with many Members. It was founded by *William Wainfleet*, the Founder of *Magdalen* College, and has in it a large Grammar School for a Nursery for *Magdalen* College. Lord Chancellor *Clarendon*, the famous Historian, who was also Chancellor of the University, was educated at this Hall.

The Late and Present GOVERNORS

Of the respective

COLLEGES and HALLS.

Late and present Presidents of Magdalen College.
1745. *Thomas Jenner*, D. D.
1768. *George Horne*, D. D.
Late and present Masters of University College.
1744. *John Browne*, D. D.
1764. *Nathan Wetherell*, D. D.
Late and present Provosts of Queen's College.
1756. *Joseph Browne*, D. D.
1767. *Thomas Fothergill*, D. D.
Late and present Wardens of All Souls College.
1726. *Stephen Niblett*, D. D.
1767. The Honourable *John Tracy*, D. D.
Late and present Principals of Brasenose College.
1770. *Ralph Cawley*, D. D.
1777. *Thomas Barker*, D. D.
Late and present Principals of Hertford College.
1757. *David Durell*, D. D.
1775. *Bernard Hodgson*, LL. D.

Late and present Wardens of New College.
1764. *Thomas Hayward*, LL. D.
1768. *John Oglander*, D. D.

Late and Present Wardens of Wadham College.
1777. *James Gerard*, D. D.
1783. *John Wills*, M. A.

Late and present Presidents of Trinity College.
1731. *George Huddesford*, D. D.
1776. *Joseph Chapman*, D. D.

Late and present Masters of Baliol College.
1721. *Joseph Hunt*, D. D.
1727. *Theophilus Leigh*, D. D.

Late and present Presidents of St. John's College.
1758. *Thomas Fry*, D. D.
1772. *Samuel Dennis*, D. D.

Late and present Provosts of Worcester College.
1736. *William Gower*, D. D.
1777. *William Sheffield*, D. D.

Late and present Rectors of Exeter College.
1750. *Francis Webber*, D. D.
1772. *Thomas Bray*, D. D.

Late and present Principals of Jesus College.
1763. *Humphrey Owen*, D. D.
1768. *Joseph Hoare*, D. D.

Late and present Rectors of Lincoln College.
1755. *Richard Hutchins*, D. D.
1782. *Charles Mortimer*, D. D.

(91)

Late and present Provosts of Oriel College.
1768. *John Clark*, D. D.
1782. *John Eveleigh*, D. D.

Late and present Presidents of Corpus Christi College.
1748. *Thomas Randolph*, D. D.
1783. *John Cooke*, D. D.

Late and present Wardens of Merton College.
1750. *John Robinson*, D. D.
1759. *Henry Barton*, D. D.

Late and present Deans of Christ Church.
1777. *Lewis Bagot*, LL. D.
1783. *Cyril Jackson*, D. D.

Late and present Masters of Pembroke College.
1738. *John Ratcliffe*, D. D.
1775. *William Adams*, D. D.

Late and present Principals of Alban Hall.
1736. *Robert Leyborne*, D. D.
1759. *Francis Randolph*, D. D.

Late and present Principals of Edmund Hall.
1751. *George Fothergill*, D. D.
1760. *George Dixon*, D. D.

Late and present Principals of St. Mary Hall.
1719. *William King*, LL. D.
1764. *Thomas Nowell*, D. D.

Late and present Principals of New Inn Hall.
1761. *William Blackstone*, LL. D.
1767. *Robert Chambers*, LL. B.

Late and present Principals of Magdalen Hall.
1744. *William Denison*, B. D.
1755. *William Denison*, D. D.

The Late and Present

Chancellors and Vice-Chancellors,

WITH THE PRESENT

Representatives in Parliament, Professors, &c.

CHANCELLORS.
1762. GEO. HENRY Earl of LITCHFIELD.
1772. FREDERICK Lord NORTH.

HIGH STEWARDS.
1763. *Hamilton*, Earl of *Cork* and *Orrery*.
1767. *Edward Leigh*, Lord *Leigh*.

VICE-CHANCELLORS.
1776. The Rev. *George Horne*, D. D. President of Magdalen College.
1780. The Rev. *Samuel Dennis*, D. D. President of St. John's College.

Present Representatives in Parliament.

Sir *William Dolben*, Bart. of Thingdon, Northamptonshire.
Francis Page, Esq; of Middle Afton, in the County of *Oxford*.

PROCTORS. 1783.
Richard Prosser, M. A. of Baliol Coll.
Charles Tahourdin, M. A. of Corpus Christi Coll.

Regius Professor of Divinity.
Rev. *John Randolph*, D. D. Canon of Christ Ch.

Margaret

Margaret Professor of Divinity.
Rev. *Timothy Neve*, D. D. of Merton College.
Regius Professor of Hebrew.
Rev. *George Jubb*, D. D. Canon of Chr. Ch.
Regius Professor of Greek.
Rev. *William Jackson*, B. D. of Christ Church.
Regius Professor of Civil Law.
Robert Vansittart, D. C. L. of All Souls College.
Vinerian Professor of Common Law.
Richard Wooddeson, LL. D. of Magdalen College.
Regius Professor of Physic.
William Vivian, M. D. of Corpus Christi College.
Regius Professor of Modern History.
Rev. *Thomas Newell*, D.D. Prin. of St. Mary Hall.
Savilian Professor of Astronomy.
Rev. *Thomas Hornsby*, M.A. of Corpus Christi Coll.
Savilian Professor of Geometry.
John Smith, M. D. of Baliol College.
Professor of Natural Philosophy.
Rev. *Thomas Hornsby*, M. A. of Corpus Christi Coll.
Professor of History.
William Scott, LL. D. of University College.
Prælector in Anatomy.
John Parsons, M. D. of Christ Church.
Prælector in Chemistry.
Martin Wall, M. D. of New College.

Professor

Professor of Botany.
Humphrey Sibthorpe, M. D. of Magdalen College.
Archbishop Laud's Professor of Arabic.
Rev. *Joseph White*, B. D. of Wadham College.
Lord Almoner's Prælector in Arabic.
Rev. *Henry Ford*, M. A. of Christ-Church.
Professor of Poetry.
Rev. *Robert Holmes*, A. M. of New College.
Professor of Music.
Philip Hayes, Doctor of Music, of Magd. Coll.
Public Orator.
James Bandinel, D. D. of Jesus College.
Radcliffe's Librarian.

Registrar of the University.
Rev. *Samuel Forster*, LL. D. of Wadham College.
Keeper of the Bodleian Library.
Rev. *John Price*, B. D. of Jesus College.
Keeper of the Ashmolean Museum.
Rev. *William Sheffield*, D. D. of Worcester College.
Keeper of the Archives.
Hon. *Thomas Wenman*, D. C. L. of All Souls Coll.

University Officers.

Esquire Beadles.
- *Robert Eyton*, M. A. of Physic and Arts.
- *James Matthews*, M. A. of Divinity.
- *Robert Paget*, LL. D. of Law.

Yeomen Beadles.
- Mr. *James Reynolds*, of Physic and Arts.
- Mr. *Robert Bliss*, of Divinity.
- Mr. *William Matthews*, of Law.

Mr. *John Green*, Clerk.
Mr. *William Court*, Virger.

A

TOUR

TO

BLENHEIM, DITCHLEY, HEYTHROP, NUNEHAM and STOW;

The SEATS of His GRACE

The Duke of MARLBOROUGH,

The Right Honourable

The Earls of LITCHFIELD, SHREWSBURY, HARCOURT and TEMPLE.

BLENHEIM CASTLE,

The Seat of his Grace the Duke of MARL-BOROUGH, near *Woodstock*.

With a Catalogue of the Paintings, Tapestry, Portraits, &c.

THE Castle of *Blenheim* is a magnificent Pile of Building; a Royal Gift to the high Merit of JOHN DUKE OF MARLBOROUGH.

From *Woodstock* (the farthest House of which on the Right Hand was the Birth-Place of the great *English* Poet *Geoffrey Chaucer*) we enter the Park through a spacious Portal of the *Corinthian* Order. The best View of the Castle is a few Paces within the Portal; where likewise are the beautiful scenes of the Park, the Bridge, the Lake, and its Valley. The Architect of the Building was Sir *John Vanbrugh*.

The Front is 348 Feet from Wing to Wing: The Roof is adorned with a Stone Balluftrade, and Statues.

The South Front is not so highly ornamented; on it is a Busto of *Louis* XIV. taken from one of the Gates of *Tournay*. The common Entrance is at the East Gate, which leads us into a Quadrangle consisting of Offices. From thence, opposite the Entrance, we proceed into the Area.

Through the superb Portico on massy Columns we enter

The HALL.

THIS magnificent Room is of the Height of the House, and of a proportionable Breadth. It is supported by *Corinthian* Pillars.

Over the Door going into the Salon,
A Buſt of John Duke of Marlborough.

Two Statues in Bronze, viz.

The Venus of Medicis, and the Fawn, Both from the Originals in Marble, in the Duke of Tuſcany's Collection at Florence, and executed by *Max. Soldani Benzi*, at Florence, 1711.

Above, upon the Right and Left, are ſeveral Marble Termini, with two excellent Statues of a Nymph and a Bacchanal.

The Cieling is painted by Sir *James Thornhill*, allegorically repreſenting Victory crowning John Duke of Marlborough, and pointing to a Plan of the Battle of Blenheim.

The Bow-Window Room.

OVER the chimney is a capital original picture of, the Virgin and Child, St. John and St. Nicholas, by *Raphael*.

This picture was brought over by the Right Hon. Lord Robert Spencer to his Brother the Duke of Marlborough, having been purchaſed by him in 1768, from the Cappela degli Anſidei at Perugia; of which Vaſari gives the following Hiſtory.——" Ritornò Raffaelle a Perugia, dove fece nella Chieſa dé Frati dé Servi in una tavola alla Cappella degli Anſidei una noſtra Donna, San Giovanni Batiſta, e San Nicola."

Over the three Doors,

A Battle Piece, by *Wouvermans*.—A St. Jerome, by *Giorgioni*.—Naked Women, by *Schiavone*.

In the pannel to the left of the chimney is a Head after Han. Caracci, by Sir *Joſhua Reynolds*.—A Head of Anne Counteſs of Sunderland, by Sir *Godfrey Kneller*.—The Aſſumption, by *Tintoret*.—A Woman's Head, by *Rubens*.—Monkies in Monk's Habits, by *Teniers*.—A Madona, by *Lionardò da Vinci*.

A TOUR TO BLENHEIM.

The Tapestry in this Room represents the Battle of Blenheim, and other Battles of John Duke of Marlborough.

The Duke's Dressing Room.

OVER the chimney, Fortune-Tellers, by *Valentino*.—A Field Marrecal, by *Cassana*.—An Academy Figure, by *Vandyck*.—Esther and Ahasuerus, by *Paulo Verones*.—Anne, Duchess of York,—Louise Renée, Duchess of Portsmouth, by Sir *Peter Lely*.—Two Landscapes, by *Wooton*.—A very scarce Day-light, by *Vandermeer*.—The Inside of a Church, by *Steenwyck*.—The Bones found in the Wilderness, by *Old Frank*.—The Circumcision of Our Saviour, by *Rembrandt*.—A small Picture, in Chalks, of the present Duchess of Marlborough, by *Gainsborough*.—A very fine Holy Family, by *Rubens*.—A Magdalen.—St. Mark writing.

Over the doors, Favourite Horses, by *Stubbs*.—And Our Saviour in the Virgin's Lap, crowning two Female Martyrs, by *Titian*.

The East Drawing-Room.

OVER the door going in from the dressing-room, is a Holy Family.—The Duchess of Buckingham and her Children by *Vandyck*.—The Marchioness de Havre, and Mary of Medicis, by *Vandyck*.—An oval Portrait of King William III. by Sir *G. Kneller*.—A French Camp, by *Watteau*.—The Annunciation, by *Corregio*.—A Landscape, by *Paul Brylle*.—An oval Portrait of the Queen Mother, by *Vandyck*.—Philip the IId, King of Spain, by *Titian*.—A very capital Bachanalian Piece, by *Rubens*.—Andromeda, by *Rubens*.—The Baptism of our Saviour, by *A Flemish Hand*.—A Man's Head, by *Holben*.—Cattle, by *Rosa di Tivoli*.—A Man's Head, by *Titian*.—The Offering of the Magi, &c. by *Rubens*.—

Rubens.—Lord Henry and Lady Charlotte Spencer, by Sir *Joshua Reynolds.*

Over the chimney.

Rubens, his Wife and Child, by *Rubens,* Given to John Duke of Marlborough by the Town of Brussels. A round Landscape,—Cattle and Figures, by *Wovermani.*—An Angel, by *Corregio.*—King Charles the Ist, by *Vandyck.*

Over the door.

A Holy Family, said to be by *Raphael,* Given to John Duke of Marlborough by the Town of *Ghent.*— Henrietta Maria, King Charles the First's Queen, by *Vandyck.*—The present Duke and Duchess of Marlborough, by *Dance.*

The Grand Cabinet.

OVER the door next to the East Drawing-Room, a Holy Family, by *Rubens.*

Over the chimney.

A Madona standing on a Globe, surrounded by Angels, by *Carlo Marratti.*—The Roman Charity, by *Rubens.*—Lot's Departure out of Sodom, by *Rubens,* Given to John Duke of Marlborough by the Town of Antwerp.

Over the other door is

The Flight into Egypt, by *Rubens.*—The Offering of the Magi, by *Rubens.*

The under row.

A very capital Picture of Our Saviour blessing the Children, by *Vandyck.*—Raphael's Mistress, exceedingly fine, by *Raphael.*—Pope Gregory, and a Female Martyr with a Palm Branch, by *Titian.*—The Portrait of Paracelsus, by *Rubens.*—A Holy Family, by *Ludovico Carracci.*—A Magdalene, in his best manner, by *Carlo Dolce.*—A Head of Rubens, by *Rubens:*

A TOUR TO BLENHEIM.

The Blue Drawing Room.
Over the two doors.

Isaac blessing Jacob, and the Woman taken in Adultery, by *Rembrandt*.—Catherine of Medicis, by *Rubens*.—Time cutting Cupid's Wings, by *Vandyck*—William Marquis of Blandford, by Sir *Godfrey Kneller*.—An Astronomer and his Family, by *Dobson*.—Our Saviour, and St John, by *Carlo Dolce*.—A Young Woman's Head, and Ditto, by *Paul Veronese*.

Under row.

Our Saviour and the Virgin in the Clouds, and a Monk worshipping, by *Hanibal Carracci*.—Our Saviour and the Virgin in the Clouds, &c. by *Tintoret*.—Thirty Miniature Portraits in one frame.—A Holy Family, by *Ludovico Carracci*.—Cattle and Figures, by *Bambocchio*.—A Landscape, by *Vanderneer*.—A Dutch Family, by *Ostade*.—A Landscape, by *Gaspard Poussin*.—Dorothy Countess of Sunderland, celebrated by Waller, by *Vandyck*.—Another Landscape, by *Gaspard Poussin*.—A small beautiful Family Piece, by *Gonzales*.—A very fine Landscape, by *Wovermans*.

The Winter Drawing-Room.

THE Tapestry is a Representation of the Cardinal Virtues.

Over the chimney is

A very fine Portrait of Mary Duchess of Richmond, and a Girl presenting her Gloves, by *Vandyck*.

Over the doors.

Lord Strafford and his Secretary, and Mrs. Killigrew and Mrs. Morton, by *Vandyck*.

The Dining Room.

OVER the door going in from the Drawing-room, is A capital Piece of Cattle and Figures, by *Castiglione*.—A Bacchanalian Piece by *Vandyck*.—Lot and his

his Daughters, by *Rubens*, Given by the Emperor.—Queen Anne, whilst Princess of Denmark, by Sir *Godfrey Kneller*.—Venus and Adonis, by *Rubens*, Given by the Emperor.—A most noble Landscape, by *Claude Lorrain*.

Over the other door.

The Rape of Europa, by *Paul Veronese*.

In the pannels near the windows, are

Six small Landscapes, by *Wootton*.

The *SALON*.

THIS Room, which is nobly decorated, is proportioned to the magnificence of the rest. The lower Part is lined with marble, which affords a cool retreat in the warmest weather.

The several compartments represent the different Nations in their various Habits and Modes of Dress, by *La Guerre*.

The cieling is emblematic, representing John Duke of Marlborough in the midst of his Victories stopt by Peace, and Time reminding him of the rapidity of his his own Flight, painted also by *La Guerre*.

Over the right-hand chimney as we enter from the hall, a Bust of *Caracalla*.

Over the other, a Bust of a Roman Consul.

Drawing Room to the Right of the Salon.

THE Tapestry represents other of John Duke of Marlborough's Battles.

Over the chimney.

A Bust of the Emperor Adrian.

Over the nearest door to the Salon, is

A Portrait of a Young Knight of St. John of Jerusalem, by *Barrocio*.

Over the opposite door.

Meleager and Atalanta, very masterly, by *Rubens*.

On the pannel near the window, next the Salon,
The Adoration of the Shepherds, by *Luca Giordano*.
Under it is,
A Madona and Child, by *Nic. Pouffin*.—A Garland of Flowers, with Figures in the middle, by *Rottenhammer*.

In the pannel opposite this is,
The Offering of the Magi, by *Luca Giordano*.—A Holy Family, by *Nic. Pouffin*.—A Garland of Flowers, with Figures in the middle, by *Rottenhammer*.—A Marble Statue of Diana on a Mahogany Therm.

Middle Drawing Room Right of the Salon.

THE Tapestry represents more of the Battles of John Duke of Marlborough.
Over the chimney.
A capital Painting upon Black Marble, by *Aleffandro Veronefe*.
Over the first door going in, is
A Picture of a Sea-Port, with a Stone Pedestal and Figures, by *Weenix*.
Over the opposite door, is
St. Lawrence distributing the Ornaments of the Altar, by *Il Prete Genoefe*.

The State Bedchamber.

ON the chimney a Bust of Diana.
Over the chimney.
A very capital Picture of Seneca bleeding to Death, by *Lucca Giordani*.
In the pannel to the left of it is,
A Portrait of King Edward VI by *Holbeins*.—A View of Architecture, by *Panini*.—The Burning of Troy, by *Old Frank*.
Over the doors.
Two Pieces of Still-life, by *Malteze*.

The LIBRARY.

FROM a series of smaller, yet magnificent Apartments, we are suddenly struck at entering this superb Room, which is 183 feet 5 inches long; in the middle it is 31 feet 9 inches wide, and at each end 28 feet 6 inches wide. The Doric Pilasters of Marble, with the complete Columns of the same, which support a rich Entablature, the Window Frames, the surrounding Basement of Black Marble, and the stuccoed Compartments of the vaulted Cieling, are in the highest taste both of Design and Finishing. It was originally intended as a Gallery for Paintings; but the late Duke adding utility to elegance, furnished it with the noble collection of books, made by Lord Sunderland, his Grace's father. Their number amounts to about 24,000 volumes, which have been allowed to be the best private collection in England.

At one end of the room is a highly finished Statue of Queen Anne, by Ryſbrack, with this Inscription,

To the Memory of Queen *ANNE,*
Under whose Auspices
JOHN Duke of *MARLBOROUGH*
Conquered
And to whose Munificence
He and his Posterity
With Gratitude
Owe the Possession of *BLENHEIM.*
A. D. MDCCXXVI.

Over the marble door, is
A Bust of Milo Crotoniensis, by *Wilton.*
Over the left-hand chimney, is
A Bust of Charles Earl of Sunderland, who collected the Books belonging to this Library.
Over each chimney are
Landscapes after *Gaspard Poussin.*

Over

A TOUR TO BLENHEIM.

Over the right-hand chimney, is
A Buſt of Charles Spencer Duke of Marlborough, by *Ryſbrac.*

At the farther End of this Room, is
A fine Greek Buſt of Alexander, in very good preſervation, on a Therm, deſigned by Sir *William Chambers.*

The Whole-length PORTRAITS are,

John Duke of Marlborough.
Sarah Duchefs of Marlborough.
Charles Duke of Marlborough.
Elizabeth Duchefs of Marlborough.
Francis Earl of Godolphin.
Anne Countefs of Sunderland.
Elizabeth Countefs of Bridgwater.
The Hon. John Spencer.
The Right Hon. Lady Georgiana Spencer, now Countefs Cowper.
John Duke of Montagu.
A Lady in Blue.

In the Galleries above ſtairs there is a large Collection of Family Portraits, by different hands.

Before we leave this Gallery, I muſt direct the Spectator to its bow-windows, from whence we have a delightful proſpect of the declivity defcending to the water, and the gradual aſcent to the groves which cover the oppoſite hill.

The CHAPEL.

THIS is one of the Wings; in which is a fuperb Monument to the memory of the Old Duke and Duchefs, by *Ryſbrack.* They are repreſented with their two fons who died young, as ſupported by Fame and Hiſtory. Beneath, in a Baſſo-relievo, is the Taking of Marſhal Tallard.

The Altar-Piece is
Our Saviour taken down from the Crofs, by *Jordans,* of *Antwerp.*

The CHINA-ROOM.

THIS Apartment, which is situated below stairs, will afford entertainment to the Curious. It is furnished with a most elegant and valuable collection of Dresden China, given to the Old Duke by the King of Poland, in return for a Pack of Stag-hounds. It consists of tureens, sets of plate, and fantastic figures. The Colours are remarkably lively, and the Representations highly natural. Here are likewise some beautiful and costly Jars, collected at a great expense by the late Duchess Dowager.

The GARDENS are spacious and agreeable: They originally consisted of about 100 acres, but the present Duke has made very large additions and elegant improvements. The noble descent to the water on the south and west, covered with flowering shrubs, and embellished with other natural beauties, will hardly be parallelled.

About the middle of the grand approach, is a magnificent BRIDGE, chiefly consisting of one arch, in the stile of the Rialto at Venice: the water is formed into a spacious lake, which covers the whole extent of a capacious valley, surrounded by an artificial declivity of a prodigious depth, and is indisputably, both with regard to its accompanyments and extent, the most capital piece of water in this kingdom.

The PARK is eleven miles in circumference, and contains many delightful scenes. The lover of rural variety will be entertained here with every circumstance of beauty, which he can expect from diversified nature; from hill and valley, water and woods.

In this Park originally stood a royal palace, where King Etheldred called a parliament. Alfred is reported to have translated *Boetius de Consolatione Philosophiæ*, while

while resident here. Henry I. inclosed the Park with a wall, the greater part of which is now remaining. His successor Henry II. principally resided at this seat, and erected in the park a house, encompassed with a Labyrinth of extraordinary contrivance, for the habitation of his concubine Fair Rosamond. This romantic retreat, commonly stiled 'Fair Rosamond's Bower, was situated in the valley, to the north-west of the bridge, near a remarkable bath, or spring, called at present Rosamond's Well.

The same King received homage in this palace, from Rice Prince of Wales, and his nobles. He likewise knighted his son Jeffery here, at his return from Normandy; And soon after he here gave his cousin, the Lady Ermengard, daughter of Richard Viscount Beaumont, in marriage to William King of Scotland.

Edmund, the second son of Edward I. was born here, and thence denominated Edmund of Woodstock; as was Edward the Black Prince. The Princess Elizabeth, afterwards Queen, was here kept a prisoner, under the persecutions of Queen Mary.

This Palace subsisted in its splendor, and was inhabited by our Kings, 'till the reign of Charles I. but began to be demolished in the succeeding times of confusion. Its magnificent ruins were remaining within the memory of man, near the bridge to the north, on the spot where two elm trees have been since planted as a memorial.

The Park and Manor of Woodstock were granted, with the concurrence of parliament, by Queen Anne, in the fourth year of her reign, to John Duke of Marlborough, and his heirs, in recompense of the many illustrious victories obtained under his command against the French and Bavarian armies; particularly at Blenheim.

The grant of the Crown, and the services of the Duke, are fully specified on the pedestal of a stately column,

column, 130 feet in height, on the top of which is a statue of the Duke, situated in the grand avenue. On one side is the following inscription, supposed to be written by the late Lord Bolingbroke.

The Castle of *Blenheim* was founded by Queen ANNE,
In the Fourth Year of her Reign,
In the Year of the Christian Æra 1705.
A Monument designed to perpetuate the Memory of the
Signal Victory
Obtained over the *French* and *Bavarians*,
Near the Village of *Blenheim*,
On the Banks of the *Danube*,
By JOHN Duke of MARLBOROUGH:
The Hero, not only of this Nation, but of this Age;
Whose Glory was equal in the Council and in the Field;
Who by Wisdom, Justice, Candour and Address,
Reconciled various, and even opposite, Interests;
Acquired an Influence,
Which no Rank, no Authority, can give,
Nor any Force but that of superior Virtue;
Became the fixed important Centre,
Which united in one common Cause,
The principal States of *Europe*;
Who by military Knowlege, and irresistable Valour,
In a long Series of uninterrupted Triumphs,
Broke the Power of *France*,
When raised the highest, when exerted the most:
Rescued the Empire from Desolation;
Asserted and confirmed the Liberties of *Europe*.

The Castle was finished at the public expense; but the bridge, the column above-mentioned, and the portal contiguous to the Town, were erected at the charge of Sarah, first Duchess-Dowager of Marlborough,

DITCHLEY,

The SEAT of the Right Honourable
The EARLS of LITCHFIELD.

DITCHLEY is a modern fabric, lofty, and elegantly built of stone, situated on an hill; which commands all the country, having Blenheim, Oxford, and the hills beyond it in full view. Over the front of the house are two grand statues, Loyalty and Fame, with their proper emblems. The offices, which form two beautiful wings, have a communication with the principal building by circular colonades. In the house are many valuable and masterly portraits by Rubens, Vandyke, Sir Peter Lely, Johnson, and Wotton.

The HALL.

This Room is finely proportioned, and elegantly decorated. Its sides and roof are ornamented with stucco, which is at once bold and delicate. Its door-cases, pediments, entablatures, and columns of the Corinthian and Composite Orders, are all richly ornamented with gildings, &c. The cieling contains an assembly of the Gods, painted by Kent. Two of the compartments are filled with historical pieces from the Æneid, by the same hand; one of which represents Æneas meeting Venus, his mother, in the Wood near Carthage; and the other, Venus presenting Æneas with the new armour. The Sciences are introduced as ornaments, with busts of philosophers, poets, historians, and orators, viz. Socrates, Virgil, Homer, Cicero, Sappho, Shakespeare, Dryden, Milton, and Livy. Over the Statues are bas-reliefs, copied from antiques out of the Florentine Museum, properly disposed; and a statue of the Venus de Medicis. And there is here a curious model of the Radclivian Library at Oxford.

The chimney-piece is superb and lofty, decorated with a portrait of the Lord Henry, by Akerman.

The MUSIC-ROOM

Has several paintings in it, viz.

The Grandfather and Grandmother of the late Earl of Litchfield.

The late Earl.

The two late Dukes of Beaufort.

The Honourable Mr. Lee, and Sir Watkin Williams Wynne, by *Hoare*, who excels in Crayons.

Rubens and his Son, hunting wild beasts.

Two Venetian Courtezans.

A Shooting-piece, and two hunting-pieces by Wotton. In the Shooting-piece, his Lordship and the Hon. Mr. Lee are introduced.

The DINING-ROOM

Is ornamented with several valuable and masterly Portraits.

Henry VIII. by *Hans Holbein*.

Charles I. with Charles II. at his Knee, by *Vandyke*.

Sir Henry Lee, with the Mastiff which once saved his life; by *Johnson*.——The story of this piece is founded on an escape of Sir Harry, from being assassinated by one of his own servants, who had formed a design of robbing the house, after having murdered his Master. But on the night it was to be put in execution,

tion, the Dog, though no favourite with, nor ever before taken notice of by his Master, accompanied him up stairs, crept under the bed, and could not be driven away by the Servant; when Sir Harry ordered him to be left: and in the dead of night, the same Servant entering the Room to execute his design, was instantly seized by the Dog, and upon being secured, confessed his intentions.

In one Corner of the Piece are the following lines.

"Mote faithful than favoured.
"Reason in Man cannot effect such Love,
"As Nature doth in them that Reason want:
"Ulysses true and kind his Dog did prove
"When Faith in better Friends was very scant.
"My Travels for my Friends have been as true,
"Tho' not as far as Fortune did him bear;
"No Friends my Love and Faith divided knew,
"Tho' neither this nor that once equall'd were.
"But in my Dog, whereof I made no Store,
"I find more Love than them I trusted more."

The late Lord by *Richardson*; and the present Dowager Lady, by *Vanderbank*, both in their Coronation-Robes.

The Duke of *Monmouth* and his Mother.
Prince *Arthur*, by *Johnson*.
Sir *Charles Rich*.
Sir *Christopher Hatton*.
Four Portraits of Sir *Henry Lee*'s Brothers, by *Cornelius Johnson*.

The DAMASK BEDCHAMBER.

The Tapestry, which is executed with uncommon Expression, represents Boys engaged in several Sports and Employments, some squeezing Grapes, others at Play, &c.

PAINT-

DITCHLEY.

PAINTINGS.

1. Admiral *Lee*.
2. The Queen of *Bohemia*, by *Johnson*.
3, 4. Lord and Lady *Tenham*.

The TAPESTRY DRAWING ROOM

Is also adorned with Tapestry, representing the Muses and *Apollo*, a Vintage and *Baccanalian* Scenes.

PAINTINGS.

1. The Countess of *Rochester*, by Sir *P. Lely*.
2. The Countess of *Lindsey*, by the same.
3. Sir *Francis Harry Lee*, by *Vandyke*.
4. Sir *Harry Lee* in the Robes of a Knight of the Garter, by *Johnson*.

In this Room we are shewn a large beautiful India Chest.

From this Apartment we have an entertaining View of a winding Valley, with a serpentine Canal, over which is thrown an elegant Bridge from a Design of *Palladio*'s.

The SALOON.

The Ceiling and Walls are richly stuccoed; in the middle Compartment of the Roof *Flora* and the Zephyrs.

ANTIQUES.

1. The Goddess Health, three Feet in Height, formerly in Dr. *Mead*'s Collection. On its Pedestal is a Bas Relief of *Æsculapius*.
2. A Medallion of a Sleeping *Cupid*. The Diameter is nine Inches.

The GREEN DAMASK DRAWING ROOM.

The marble Chimney Piece and Table in this Room are

DITCHLEY. 113

are of the moſt beautiful Sorts. The two *Corinthian* Columns to the Chimney Piece and high finiſhing of the Whole, are worthy of *Scheemaker*, who was the Artiſt.

The Landſcape in the middle is by Mr. *Wotton*, who has gained great Applauſe in this Species of Painting.

A rich japanned Cabinet, with two gilt Stands, and ſuperb gilt Branches on each of them.

GILT DRAWING ROOM.

This was formerly called the Beſt Dining Room.

PAINTINGS.

A full-length Portrait of *Charles* II. and of the Dutcheſs of *Cleveland*, by *Lely*.

The preſent Duke of *Grafton*'s Great Grandfather, And Lady *Charlotte Fitzroy*, his Lordſhip's Grandmother, by *Kneller*.

The Decorations of the Wainſcot are gilt; and the ſtuccoed Cieling is correſpondent to the Taſte and Splendor of the reſt.

Here are two Tables of *Ægyptian* Marble, which juſtly demand our Obſervation.

The Chimney Piece of this Apartment is alſo executed by *Scheemaker:* In the Freeze a *Bacchanalian*'s Head finely executed; and over it a Landſcape by *Wotton*.

The VELVET BEDCHAMBER,

So called from the Bed and Hangings, which are of a ſingular Figure.

The elegant Chimney Piece is by *Scheemaker*, ornamented with an *Italian* Proſpect of a Ruin.

The Dreſſing Table is of Tortoiſe-Shell, curiouſly inlaid. It was made in *France*, and muſt have been a Work of Labour.

DITCHLEY.

The TAPESTRY ROOM

Is the last we are shewn, curiously ornamented in the *Chinese* Taste, and has two elegant and costly Sconces.

The Tapestry represent the *Cyclops* forging the Armour for *Æneas*, and *Neptune*, properly attended, directing the refitting a Vessel, which has been shipwrecked.

The Chimney Piece is of white Marble. Over it is a capital Picture by Sir *Peter Lely* of the Duke and Dutchess of *York*, and the Princesses *Mary* and *Anne*.

Two Landscapes over the Doors are by an *Italian* Master.

The Chairs in this Room are each ornamented with one of the Fables of *Æsop*.

In this Apartment is a beautiful Fire-Screen of Needle Work, by the Dowager Lady *Litchfield*. The Subject is the Rape of *Proserpine*.

Proper to this Apartment are the *Chinese* Lady and the Porter with a Chest of Tea. Two rich Branches on each Side the Chimney-Piece; one supported by a *Black-moor*, the other by a *Mullatto*.

HEYTHROP,

The Seat of the Right Honourable

The EARL of SHREWSBURY.

IT is situated seventeen miles north of Oxford, and about four and an half from the Seat of the Earl of Litchfield. It stands on an eminence, and has every delight that can result from a diversity of Wood, Water, Eminences, and Vales.

An Avenue of above two miles, planted on each side with Forest Trees, interspersed with Clumps of Fir, leads from the North to the grand Area before the House; and by its length and variety, forms an exceeding magnificent Approach.

The House is a regular Edifice, consisting of four Fronts, built in a most elegant stile of Architecture, and is joined to the Offices by open Arcades. Tho' this beautiful Structure was finish'd but 70 Years ago, and tho' the whole Spot was an open and rather uncultivated Country, the advanced Growth of the Trees, and beautiful Verdure, gives it an Appearance equal to any. We enter the House by a Flight of steps under a grand Portico, supported by four lofty Corinthian Columns.

The HALL,

IS a well-proportioned Room, thirty-two feet by twenty-seven feet nine. It is finished in plain Stucco, and adorned with Vases and Lamps. The eye is agreeably surprized on first entring, by the reflection of the Avenue, and part of the Hall, from two large sashes on each side the door leading to the Salon, which, raises the idea of another room of equal dimensions and magnificence.

From the Hall, we go to the grand Staircase, the walls and cieling of which are ornamented with Pannels and Festoons of Stucco. We next come to

The BREAKFASTING PARLOUR,

A Neat and commodious Room. Over the chimney is a fine Landscape by Poussin; and four other Landscapes, by an eminent Italian Master; as likewise an excellent Portrait of some unknown Person, by Hans Holben: with some other Landscapes and Portraits.

From hence we pass to

The BLUE DRAWING ROOM.

THIS is an apartment of 21 feet by 18½, and enriched with an elegant Chimney-piece, of Sienna Marble, executed by the late Mr. Carter.

Over the Chimney is a piece of King Charles II. by Vandyke; and on the sides of the Room the Portraits of the present Earl and Countess of Shrewsbury, by Mr. Hoare.

His Lordship's BED CHAMBER;

IS fitted up with tapestry, with a rich blue damask Bed and Furniture. Next to it is

Her Ladyship's DRESSING ROOM;

AN elegant Apartment, hung with Chinese Paper; from whence we command an extensive Prospect over the adjacent Country.

From the Bed Chamber before mentioned we come to

The LIBRARY,

WHICH is a superb Room, 83 feet in length, and 20 in height.

The Ornaments of this Room are masterly: They consist chiefly of the most elegant and highly finished Stucco, by the late and present Mr. Roberts of Oxford;—the Designs of which are admirably adapted to the purposes of the place.

On the north side are seven Recesses, one of which is the entrance from the Hall, and the other six are filled with elegant Book-cases, over which are curious Medalions of Cicero, Plato, Thucidides, Homer, Shakespeare, and Inigo Jones. In this side are also two superb Chimney-pieces, by Carter, composed of rich antique Marble. The Entrances at each end are formed to correspond with the other Recesses; the semicircular Arches over which, as well as that leading from the Hall, are ornamented in Stucco with Fables from Æsop, admirably executed; and a Medalion of the same kind over each Chimney. The south side, which fronts the Garden, consists of eight magnificent windows, with a pair of folding Glass Doors, which open to the Terras, and afford a most delightful and extensive Prospect.

The cieling, which is entirely plain, is supported by Columns of the Corinthian Order; and is encompassed by an exceeding rich Ionic Entablature. This Room is likewise enriched by pendant Ornaments, in alto relievo, of Still-life, Military, Musical, and Mathematical

tical Inftruments; with a judicious mixture of Fruit and Flowers.

The BREAKFASTING PARLOUR,

IS furnifhed with Genoa Flowered Damafk, and has a Chimney-piece of fine Mable, and very curious workmanfhip. The Cieling and Cove are in fret-work Compartments, ornamented with Birds, Foliages, and Feftoons of Flowers.

The GREAT DRAWING ROOM.

THIS Apartment is 47 feet long, 25 broad, and 20 high. It is furnifhed with Tapeftry, which for Colour as well as Expreffion, engages the attention of the Curious. It is the work of Vanderborght, and reprefents the Four Quarters of the World, well expreffed by Affemblages of the Natives, in their various Habits and Employments, except Europe, which is in Mafquerade. Over the four doors are the Seafons and Elements painted in a very peculiar ftyle. Thefe figures, in Claro Obfcuro, appear as if ftarting from the Canvas. From the vaft expreffion, yet exceeding light tint of thefe Pieces, the Spectator is at firft fight ready to pronounce them Bas Reliefs in white Marble.

The Chimney-piece is extremely fuperb, compofed of rich Egyptian Marble, executed by Carter. The Cornice is fupported by highly carved and polifhed Figures of Ceres and Flora, about five feet high: The Drapery of thefe Figures, one in the ancient, the other in the modern ftyle, as well as their Attitudes, are peculiarly ftriking and expreffive. In the centre of the Freeze is a raifed Tablet of the Choice of Hercules. Over it is a Painting of the Deftruction of Pharaoh and his Hoft in the Red Sea.—Suitable to the other Ornaments of this Apartment, the Cieling confifts of reprefentations of the Four Quarters of the World,

with

with the Elements, and Seasons, in Stucco, interspersed with Fables and other decorations; and surrounded by a full enriched Corinthian Entablature.—On the opposite side to the Chimney-piece are two superb Glasses, upwards of four feet in breadth, and nine feet high.— Under these glasses are two rich Tables of Egyptian Marble, upon gilt and carved frames; and on the other Piers are two Girandoles of exquisite workmanship, by Ansell.

The Settees and Chairs of this well proportioned and highly decorated Apartment are richly carved and gilt, the seats of which are covered with needlework in silk, representing different bunches of Flowers: here are also two curious Fire skreens, by the same hand as the Tapestry; one exhibits a Dutch Merriment, the other Sportsmen returned from shooting, with their Game.

The MUSICK PARLOUR,

IS a small neat Room, with a light and well executed Cieling.

The DINING PARLOUR.

A Very commodious Apartment, of 27 feet, by 25. The Walls, with the Cove and Cieling, are decorated with varied compartments of highly finished Ornaments, in Stucco. Over the Chimney, is a Portrait of the late Duke of Shrewsbury.

The Environs, or Gardens, are well laid out. A variety of beautiful Scenes strike the Spectator in a most agreeable Succession. With very little appearance of Art, Nature has received much Assistance from Taste. To the South West, lofty trees afford a most refreshing shade, interspersed with Openings edged with Flowers. Eastward, a small stream is improved into a winding River, broke by Cafcades, whofe banks are adorned with a curious Fancy-building called

The HERMITAGE.

IT is covered with Reeds, and conftructed of ruftic Oak; the infide is lined with Mofs of various colours, and the floor is paved, in Mofaic-work, with teeth polifhed. Upon entering this Building we have a ftriking view of two Cafcades, which afford an agreeable furprize.

This piece of Water is croffed by a ftone Bridge, under which is an Engine that fupplies the houfe with water; and above it, at the diftance of about 400 paces, is the moft natural, if not the moft ftriking of the Cafcades found here. It is built with Petrefactions and other curious Stones.

From this Bridge, in another direction, we afcend to a grafs Terrace, planted with Flowering Shrubs on each fide, that terminates in an octagon Bowling-green, where we command feveral extenfive and different Profpects.

NUNEHAM.

NUNEHAM,

The SEAT of

The EARL of HARCOURT.

IN this House, which is a modern Fabrick, the rooms throughout have arched Cielings, to prevent the fatal effects of fire; and the roof is covered with copper. There are two detached Wings for the Offices, and the Stabling and Coach Houses are thrown back to a confiderable diftance.

This Seat is placed on the fide of a Hill, about two furlongs from the River *Thames*, upon fo elevated a fituation as to command a very extenfive profpect, particularly on the *Berkshire* fide; and from the Windows of the Octagon Room, it is fcarce poffible to conceive a Profpect more highly enriched. The Eye is delighted with a fine meandring River for many Miles; at a proper diftance rifes the Town of *Abingdon*; and, as a capital Object, which bounds the fight northward, we have a full View of *Oxford*. Exclufive of thefe, there are not wanting the rural Charms afforded by a neighbouring Country interfperfed with Villages, Wood, and Water, rich Meadows, and fruitful Hills.

The Houfe is encompaffed by a very extenfive Park, planted, and laid out with Tafte, by the late Earl; in which is included a noble Terrace, and a delightful Pleasure Garden: And upon an Eminence nearly contiguous to the House, the Parish Church has been rebuilt by his Lordship, of curious Masonry, and constructed in the form of a Roman Temple.

The furniture of the House is elegant, and enriched with many capital PAINTINGS.

The BREAKFAST ROOM.

Over the Chimney; a Nymph with Cupids, representing Evening, by Valerio Castelli.

Over one Door; Mary Daughter of Sir William Waller, Knight.

Over the other; The Honourable Simon Harcourt, only Son of Simon first Vicount Harcourt; painted at Paris, by Le Bel.

Robert, eldest Son of Sir Walter Harcourt, Knight. He was the principal adventurer, with Sir Walter Ralegh, in his Voyage to Guiana, and at his own expence, built and fitted out three ships for that expedition.

A Landscape with large Figures, a fine Picture, by Francesco Bolognese.

Two Landscapes by Tempesta of Genoa.

VELVET BED CHAMBER.

Over the Chimney; a Picture of Architecture, with Figures, by Viviani.

Over one Door; Sir Simon Harcourt, Knight, eldest Son of Robert: he was Governor of Dublin in the year 1642, and killed at the Seige of Carrickmain in 1643.

Over the other; Ann, Daughter of William 4th Lord Paget, Wife to Sir Simon Harcourt.

King George the third, by Ramsay.

TAPESTRY

TAPESTRY DRESSING ROOM.

Over the Chimney; Francis second Son of Robert Harcourt.

Over one Door; the Lady Ann Finch, Daughter of Sir Thomas Finch, Bart. and second Earl of Winchelsea, Wife to Sir William Waller, General of the Parliament Army.

Over the other; William Lord Paget.

The EATING ROOM.
32 by 24, and 18½ feet high.

Over the Chimney; Ulysses and Nausicaa, a most capital Picture by Salvator Rosa; a present to Lord Harcourt, from the Duke de Harcourt.

A Landscape by Ruysdaal, the figures by Wouvermans.

Dead Game, and Dogs, very fine, by Snyder.

Two views of Rome and Naples, by Gasper Occhiali.

Over one door; Dead Game by Murillio, from the Collection of Mr. Bagnols.

Over the other; the Cascade of Terni, by Orizonti.

A large and fine Landscape with Figures and Cattle, by Rosa of Tivoli.

Two Pictures of the Ruins of Rome with Figures by Paolo Panini. Painted for Lord Harcourt.

A Landscape, with Figures, and Cattle, by Cuyp, from the Collection of Lord Kingsland, at Dublin.

Two fruit Peices by Michael Angelo Campidoglio.

A Herdsman and Cattle by Murillio, a curious Picture, from the Collection of Mr. Bagnols.

An Evening, with a Shepherd and Sheep, highly finished by Bamboccio.

Two large, and fine Landscapes, by Van Artois, the figures by David Teniers, from the Collection of Mr. Bagnols.

The OCTAGON.
30 by 24, and 18½ feet high.

On one fide of the Chimney; the Nativity by Bronzino.

Under it; the Madonna and Child, very beautiful, by Guido, bought out of the Hotel de Hautefort at Paris.

The Holy Family, a celebrated Picture of Barocci, and known by the name of La Madonna della Gatta, from the Cat in one corner. It has been etched, by Barocci himfelf. From the Collection of the Earl of Pomfret.

A Moon-light on the Water, a perfect Picture of Vander Neer.

Mars, Venus, and Cupids, by Niccolo Pouffin, capital; from the Collection of Mr. Furnefe.

A Landfcape, with Ruins, beautiful, by Patel; from the Collection of Monfieur de La Live at Paris.

A Landfcape by Gafparo Pouffin.

A View of the Rhine, by Vofterman, very rare.

Mofes fweetening the Waters of Marah, highly coloured, by Niccolo Pouffin.

A Landfcape with a Cart overturning by Moon light, a Capital Picture by Rubens, and well known by Bolfwaert's Print called La Charrette embourbée; from the Collection of the Comte de Guiche.

The following fix Pictures hang on either fide of the Rubens, and are fmall.

The Trinity, painted on a Gold Ground, by Andrea del Sarto, a prefent to Lord Harcourt from Mr. Knapton.

St. Cecilia lying dead, and two Boy-Angels, exquifitely painted by Dominichino.

A beauti-

A beautiful and moſt lively Portrait of Sophoniſba Anguſciola, by Herſelf, from the Collection of Mr. Bagnols.

Spring, with four Cupids, a ſweet Picture, by Filippo Laura; a preſent from William Fauquier Eſq;

Chriſt crowned with Thorns by Alleſſandro Veroneſe.

The Holy Family, by Rottenhamer, in the ſtyle of the old Italian Maſters, from the Collection of Mr. Fauquier.

Over one Door; Noah's Sacrifice, the Ark at a diſtance, by Imperiali.

Two beautiful Pictures of Ruins and Figures, by Filippo Laura, from the Collection of Dr. Mead.

Over the other Door; a fine Landſcape, with Figures, by Both.

Chriſt driving the money changers out of the Temple, by Baſſano.

The Holy Family, by Albano.

Two ſmall and highly finiſhed Views, of the Rhine, by Old Griffier.

The SALON.
49 by 24, and 18½ feet high.

St. Margaret, whole length, a moſt capital, and highly preſerved Picture, by Titiano. It was in the Collection of King Charles the firſt, and has been etched by H. Howard.

Joſeph and Potiphar's wife, by Franceſcini, after Carlo Cignani.

A Farm Yard, with Figures and Cattle, by Murillio, from the Collection of Mr Bagnols.

St. John preaching in the Wilderneſs, by Albano, from the Collection of the Earl of Waldegrave.

A Woman on Horſeback, with ſeveral Figures, and Animals, by Watteau.

A Landſcape, with Figures, and Cattle, by Van Uden.   A fine

A fine and bright Landscape, with buildings, by Gasparo Poussin; the Figures by Niccolo.

A very fine Landscape, and Figures, by Niccolo Poussin, from the Collection of Mr. Houlditch; it has been engraved by Vivares.

Two other large Landscapes by Van Artois, the Figures in one, by David Teniers; from the Collection of Mr. Bagnols.

The Holy Family by le Sueur, very fine.

Louis XIV. on Horseback attended by his Court.

An entertainment on the Texel, with English and Dutch Yatchts, a capital Vandervelde.

Over one Door, two Begger Boys, by Murillo; It came from Penshurst.

Over the other, Susanna and the Elders, by Anibale Carracci.

On the left side of the Venetian Window.

A Landscape by Wootton.

A Landscape with a Cottage by Decker.

A Landscape by Claude Le Lorrain, in his first manner.

On the right side.

A Landscape by Wootton.

A Landscape and Figures, by Van Goyen.

A Landscape by Ruysdaal.

ANTI CHAMBER.

Frederick, second Son of Sir Simon Harcourt.

Elizabeth, eldest Daughter of the Honourable Simon Harcourt, by Zeeman.

Over the Chimney.

Frances, Daughter of Geoffrey Vere, youngest Son of John Earl of Oxford, Wife to Robert Harcourt.—

On the left side.

Ann, Daughter of Simon Vicount Harcourt, wife to
John

John Barlow Efq; of Slebech in Pembrokeshire. By Kneller.

Sir Philip Harcourt, Eldeſt Son of Sir Simon, after Cowper.

On the right ſide,

Elizabeth, Daughter of John Evelyn Efq; of Wotton in Surry; wife to the Honourable Simon Harcourt, by Dahl.

Anne, Daughter of Sir William Waller, wife to Sir Philip Harcourt——after Mrs. Beale.

Over one Door; Michael ſecond Son of Sir Walter Harcourt, commander of one of his Brother Robert's Ships, in Sir Walter Ralegh's Expedition.

The LIBRARY.

Over the Chimney, Simon, only Son of Sir Philip, Baron (afterwards Vicount) Harcourt, Lord high Chancellor.

Over one Door; Simon Earl Harcourt in the Robes of the Lord Lieutenant of Ireland, by Hunter of Dublin.

Over the other; Rebecca, Daughter and heireſs of Charles Le Bas, of Pipwell Abbey, in Northamptonſhire, wife to Simon Earl Harcourt; by Knapton,

DESCRIPTION of the FLOWER GARDEN at NUNEHAM.

THIS small spot contains only about an acre and a quarter; but from the irregularity of its form, the inequality of the ground, and the disposition of the trees, it appears of considerable extent. The boundary is concealed by a deep plantation of shrubs, which unites with the surrounding forest trees that stand in the park. The garden is laid out in patches of flowers and clumps of shrubs, of unequal dimensions, and various shapes, and a gravel walk leads round it, to the different buildings and busts, on which are the following inscriptions.

Fronting the Gate, a Bust of Flora on a Term.

Here springs the Violet all newe,
And fresh perwinke riche of hewe;
And Flouris yalowe white and rede,
Such plenti grew ther ner in mede:
Ful gai is all the grounde, & queint,
And poudrid, as men had it peint,
With many a fresh and sondry floure
That castin up ful gode favoure.   CHAUCER.

COWLEY.

When Epicurus to the world had taught,
  That pleasure was the chiefest good,
His life he to his doctrine brought,
  And in a garden's shade, that sovereign pelasure sought.   COWLEY.

The

The GROTTO.

—————— Musing meditation most affects
The pensive secrecy of desert cell,
—————————————— and wisdom's self
Oft seeks to sweet retired solitude,
Where with her best nurse, contemplation,
She plumes her feathers, and lets grow her wings,
That in the various bustle of resort,
Were all too ruffled, and sometimes impair'd.
MILTON.

APOLLO.

Lucido Dio,
Per cui l' April fiorisce. METASTASIO.

The Temple of FLORA.

On one side a Bust of FAUNUS.

Faunus would oft, as Horace sings,
  Delighted with *his* rural seats,
Forsake Arcadia's groves and springs,
  For soft Lucretile's retreats.
'Twas beauty charm'd! what wonder then,
  Enamour'd of a fairer scene,
The changeful god should change again,
  And *here*, for ever fix his reign!
WM. WHITEHEAD, Esq.

On the other, a Bust of PAN.

Here universal Pan,
Knit with the graces, and the hours in dance,
Leads on th' eternal spring. MILTON.

VENUS.

VENUS.

Thee, goddess, thee the clouds and tempests fear,
And at thy pleasing presence disappear:
For thee the land in fragrant flow'rs is dress'd.
DRYDEN, from Lucretius.

The BOWER.
In which is the following Inscription.

Fair Quiet, have I found thee here,
With innocence thy sister dear!
Mistaken long, I sought thee then,
In busy companies of men:
Your sacred plants, at length I know,
Will only in retirement grow.
Society is all but rude,
To this delicious solitude,
Where all the trees and flowrets close,
To weave the garland of repose.
ANDREW MARVEL.

On one side a Bust of CATO, of Utica,

A' ce nom saint, & auguste, tout ami de la vertu
Doit mettre le front dans la poussiere, & honorer
En silence la memoire du plus grane des hommes.
J. J. ROUSSEAU.

On the other,
A Bust of J. J. ROUSSEAU.

Say, is thy honest heart to virtue warm!
Can genius animate thy feeling breast!
Approach, behold this venerable form;
'Tis Rousseau! let thy bosom speak the rest.
BR. BOOTHBY, Esq.

NUNEHAM. *Flower Garden.*

PRIOR.

See friend, in some few fleeting hours,
　See yonder what a change is made!
Ah me! the blooming pride of May,
　And that of beauty, are but one;
At morn, both flourish bright and gay,
　Both fade at evening, pale and gone.　　PRIOR.

The URN,

Sacred
to the memory of Frances Poole, Viscountess Palmerston.

Here shall our ling'ring footsteps oft be found,
This is *Her* shrine, and consecrates the ground.
Here living sweets around her altar rise,
And breathe perpetual incense to the skies.
　Here too the thoughtless and the young may tread,
Who shun the drearier mansions of the dead;
May here be taught what worth the world has known,
Her wit, her sense, her virtues were her own;
To her peculiar—and for ever lost
To those who knew, and therefore lov'd her most.
　O! if kind pity steal on virtue's eye,
Check not the tear, nor stop the useful sigh;
From soft humanity's ingenuous flame
A wish may rise to emulate her fame,
And some faint image of her worth restore,
When those, who now lament her, are no more.

G^e. S^r. Harcourt, and the Hon. Eliz. Vernon, Vic^t.
and Vic^{tss}. Nuneham, erected this urn in the year 1771.
Wm. Whitehead, Esq. Poet Laureat, wrote the Verses.

On the right side of the Garden,
back'd by a Plantation of Shrubs,
is a Bust of LOCKE,

Who made the whole internal world his own,
Who shew'd confess'd to reason's purged eye,
That nature's first best gift was Liberty.

The CONSERVATORY,

Fifty feet by fifteen, is planted with bergamot, cedrati, Limoncelli, and orange trees of various kinds and sizes. In summer, the front, sides, and roof of the building are entirely removed, and the trees appear in the natural ground. The back wall is covered with a treillage, against which are planted lemon, citron, and pomegranate trees, intermixed with all the different sorts of jessamines.

The Statue of HEBE

terminates the principal glade, and fronts the temple of Flora: it is backed by a large clump of shrubs, which forms a collection of all such ever-greens as flourish in the open air. On the pedestral of the statue are the following verses:

Hebe, from thy cup divine,
Shed, O! shed, nectareous dews,
Here o'er Nature's living shrine,
Th' immortal drops diffuse:
Here while every bloom's display'd,
Shining fair in vernal Pride,
Catch the colours e'er they fade,
And check the green blood's ebbing tide,
Till youth eternal like thine own prevail,
Safe from the night's damp wing or day's infidious gale.

WM. WHITEHEAD, Esq.

THE
House and Gardens at STOW,

The SEAT of
The Right Hon. the Earl TEMPLE.

A Grand Flight of Steps, designed by *Signor Borra*, ornamented with Balustrades, leads us to

The SALOON,

WHICH is a grand Apartment hung with Tapestry, representing the Functions of the Cavalry. The Dimensions of this Room are 43 Feet by 22; the Furniture is Crimson, ornamented with two Marble Busts, a rich Cabinet, and fine *China* Jars.

The PICTURES are
1. A Landscape.
2. A Flower-piece.
3. A Fruit-piece.

The HALL.

THIS is a spacious Room, 36 Feet by 22 and half, designed and painted by *Kent*. It's Cieling is enriched with the Signs of the *Zodiac*; and the Walls are adorned with Festoons of Flowers, &c.

Over the Chimney is a curious Piece of Alto Relievo, the Story of which is *Darius's* Tent: Here are also eleven Marble Busts, properly disposed, and a Statue of *Narcissus*.

The DINING ROOM

IS a well proportioned Apartment, 30 feet by 21, in which are the following Paintings, viz.

Two large Landscapes, by *Orizonti*.
Two small ditto, by *Loten*.
A Dancing at the Duke of *Mantua*'s Marriage, by *Tintoretto*.
A Landscape, by *Claude Lorrain*.
A small ditto of *Acis* and *Galatea*, by *Milé*.
A large Picture of young *Bacchanals*.
A Sea Port, by a *Flemish* Master.
A Landscape with Figures and Cattle, by *Bassan*.
A Landscape, with a Mill.
Vulcan, and *Venus*.
The Marriage at *Cana*, by *Bassan*.
Moses burying the *Ægyptian*, by *Poussin*.

A Bed Chamber, with two Dressing Rooms.

THE Hangings, Bed, and Furniture of this Apartment are rich Crimson; and over the Chimney is a full length Portrait of the late Countess of *Dorset*.

In the first Dressing Room, a Piece of Still Life over the Chimney.

In the Second, a fine Cabinet, and over the Chimney, Prince *Henry*, at full length.

The Grand STAIR CASE.

THIS Stair Case is ornamented with Iron Work, and enriched with three Cieling-pieces, painted by *Sclater*, viz.

1. Justice and Peace.
2. Fame and Victory.
3. Plenty and Constancy.

The Walls are adorned with military Pieces.

The CHAPEL

IS wainscotted with Cedar, and has a Gallery of the same, hung with Crimson Velvet. Its Dimensions are, 37 Feet by 20 Feet 10 Inches, and 26 Feet high.

Over the Communion Table is a fine Painting of the Resurrection, by *Tintoretto*; and over that is the King's Arms, richly carved and ornamented.

Above the Cedar Wainscot, are the following Paintings at full length, viz.

1. *Moses* and *Aaron*.
2. St. *Peter* and St. *Paul*.
3. The Four Evangelists.
4. The Ascension.
5. Baptism.
6. The Salutation of the Virgin *Mary*.

The Cieling is the same as in the Chapel Royal at St. *James's*, and the Cedar Wainscot enriched with elegant Carving, by *Guibbons*.

Her Ladyship's Dressing Room.

THE Hangings, Chairs, and Window Curtains of fine printed Cotton.

A fine old *Japan* Cabinet, ornamented with China Jars.

A fine View of *Pekin*, over the Chimney-Piece, by *Iolli*.

Her Ladyship's Bed-Chamber.

THE Hangings, Chairs, &c. the same as the Dressing Room; with a Picture of a *Chinese* Temple over the Chimney, by *Iolli*.

The CHINESE CLOSET.

THIS is the Repository of her Ladyship's valuable China. The Japan and Ornaments were a Present from the late Prince and Princess of *Wales*.

From hence we enter a Colonade adorned with Paintings, by *Sclater*. It is embellished with Exotics and flowering Shrubs.

The GRENVILLE ROOM,

IS 29 Feet 8 Inches by 26 Feet 3 Inches, and 19 Feet 4 Inches high, is hung with Green Velvet, and ornamented with the following Portraits, all at full length, except the first.

1. The late Countess *Temple*, Mother to the present Earl.
2. The present Countess *Temple*.
3. The present Earl *Temple*.
4. The Right Honourable *George Grenville*.
5. The Honourable *James Grenville*.
6. The Honourable *Henry Grenville*, formerly Governor of *Barbadoes*.
7. The Honourable *Thomas Grenville*, who was killed in Defence of his Country, on board the *Defiance*, of which Ship he was Captain.
8. The Right Honourable Lady *Hester Pitt*.

The GALLERY.

A Magnificent Apartment, 74 Feet by 25 Feet, and 20 Feet high, with Gobelin Tapestry Chairs, and is hung with three fine Pieces of Tapestry, viz.

1. A beautiful Representation of a Farm.
2. A *Dutch* Wake from *Teniers*.
3. A *Dutch* Fishery, from ditto.

The two Chimnies have Pictures of *Roman* Ruins over each, by *Panini*.

The Four Doors have rural Pictures over each, viz.

1. Plowing. 2. Reaping.
3. Hay-making. 4. Sheep-shearing.

And a Rich Cabinet at each End, containing Books; and 10 Marble Busts of *Roman* Emperors.

A Dressing-Room.

HANGINGS of Yellow Silk Damask, trimmed with Silver; with the following Paintings:
Joan of *Arc*, over the Chimney.
Sir *Thomas Temple*.
Lady *Hester Temple*.

A Bed-Chamber.

THE Hangings, Bed, Chairs and Ornaments of Yellow Damask, the same as in the Dressing-Room; with Paintings of,
The Representation of the *Holy Lamb*.
A Flower Piece.
Two Landscapes, one over each Door.

A Dressing-Room.

GREEN Damask, trimmed with Gold, with the following Paintings.
A Picture over the Chimney, by *Rembrant*.
Two Saints, St. *Laurence*, and St. *Stephen*, one over each Door.
On one Side, *Orodes* ordering melted Gold to be poured into the Mouth of *Crassus*.
On the other, two Pieces of Ruins, and a Landscape, with Dancing Satyrs, by *Paul Brill*.
The Rape of *Helen*, by *Theseus*.
The Return of *Chryseis* to her Father; both by *Primaticcio*.

A Bed-Chamber.

GREEN Damask Bed, Hangings and Chairs trimmed with Gold.

PAINTINGS.

1. An Original Portrait of *Oliver Cromwell*.
2. A *Silenus*.
3. A Portrait of Colonel *Stanyan*.

A Dressing-Room.

THE Paintings in this Room are,
A Portrait of *Rubens*'s Wife, over one Door, by *Rubens*.

Over the other, a Knight of the Bath, by *Vandyke*.
Cymon and *Iphigenia*.

The STATE APARTMENTS.

The State Gallery;
Is 70 Feet 9 Inches, by 25 Feet long, and 22 Feet high;

WITH two Marble Chimney Pieces of *Sienna*, &c. The Cieling finely ornamented with Paintings and Gilding, by *Sclater*. Two fine large Marble Tables, with two large Pier-Glasses.——The Walls are adorned with curious Pieces of Tapestry, viz.
1. The Triumph of *Diana*.
2. The Triumph of *Mars*.
3. The Triumph of *Venus*.
4. The Triumph of *Bacchus*.
5. The Triumph of *Ceres*.

The Piers are adorned with Trophies.

Two Chimnies, the upper Parts of which are adorned with Gilding and Carving.
1. Representing *Mercury*, conducting Tragic and Comic Poetry to the Hill of *Parnassus*.
2. A Goddess conducting Learning to Truth.

The State Dressing-Room
Is 24 Feet 8 Inches, by 30 Feet, and 19 Feet 4 Inches high;

HUNG with Blue Damask, and Chairs and Window Curtains of the same. The Doors and Cieling

ing are finely ornamented with Carving and Gilding.
The Paintings are,

A fine Portrait of the late Lord *Cobham*, by Sir *Godfrey Kneller*.

Four Conversation Pieces, by *Francisco Cippo*.

Venus binding the Eyes of a Cupid, and the Graces offering Tribute.

The State Bed-Chamber.

Is 56 Feet 8 Inches, by 25 Feet 10 Inches, and 18 Feet 8 Inches high.

THE Bed and Cieling by *Signor Borra*; and Pillars of the Corinthian Order: The whole finely carved and gilt.

A Madona from the School of Rubens.

A Picture over the Chimney.

A very Curious Chimney-piece of White Marble, designed by Signor Borra.

Two Marble Tables.

Two fine large Pier Glasses.

The State Closet.

HUNG with Blue Damask, finely ornamented with Carving and Gilding.——Out of which we go into a Colonade, where is a beautiful View of the Gardens and the Country. The Passage is ornamented with Marble Busts.

There is also a grand Stair-case, adorned with Paintings of the Four Seasons.——The Cieling represents the Rising Sun, by *Phœbus* in his Car.

The GARDENS.

THE Spectator will have an Idea of what he is to expect in these unrivalled Gardens, where

Art

Art and Nature are so excellently blended, by the following Lines.

With Envy stung, and Emulation fir'd,
Nature and *Art*, each separately aspir'd
To guide the Pleasures of th' admiring Few
In Objects great, or beautiful, or new.

Nature the Forest plants, extends the Plain,
Paints the Blue Hill, and spreads the glassy Main:
Here length'ned Views allow the Eye to range;
More bounded Prospects there the Landskip change.
Art bids; and, lo! obedient Cities rise,
And glittering Spires shoot upwards to the Skies:
Its pompous Bulk the splendid Palace rears,
And each gay Order on its Front appears.

Separate these Rivals thus aspire to Fame,
But each misguided, lost her purpos'd Aim.
All cry aloud, when *Nature's* Works appear,
What vast Extravagance, what Wildness here!
Nor pleas'd with *Art* alone, each Eye can see
Stiffness in her, and trim Formality.

Baffled in each Attempt, at Length they cease
Their fierce Dispute, and knit in Leagues of Peace;
Determin'd with associate Powers to shew
One Matchless Effort of their Force at STOW.

The World, astonish'd, as the Labour grew,
Exclaims, " What cannot *Art* and *Nature* do!"

The Southern entrance of the Gardens is formed by two Pavillions of the Doric order, designed by Sir *John Vanbrugh*. They are adorned with Rough masterly Paintings, by *Nollikins*. The Stories are from *Pastor Fido*.*

The first striking Object is an OBELISC, near 70 Feet high, designed for a Jet d'Eau, and placed in the Middle of a large OCTAGON PIECE OF WATER. At some Distance we perceive two Rivers, which are at

---

* Act ii, Scene 3.———Act iii, Scene 2.

laſt united, and enter the OCTAGON in one ſtream. Over one of theſe is a PALLADIAN BRIDGE. From this point a Gothic Edifice dedicated to Liberty, 70 feet in height, appears on the top of a hill. On the left is an ÆGYPTIAN PYRAMID. Here we have a Proſpect of a natural CASCADE, falling from the laſt mentioned OCTAGON, in three diſtinct ſheets, into an extenſive LAKE. One of them paſſes through the arch of an ARTIFICIAL RUIN, covered with ever-greens.

But it is time to drop this general and collective detail, and proceed to give a circumſtantial and diſtinct diſplay of each remarkable Particular, as it ſeverally and ſucceſſively preſents itſelf, in our progreſs through the Gardens.

The HERMITAGE, built of rough ſtone and agreeably ſituated in a riſing Wood, on the banks of the Lake.

The STATUES of CAIN and ABEL, which are finely executed.

The TEMPLE of VENUS, with the Inſcription, VENERI HORTENSI; i. e. "*To the Garden Venus.*" It was deſigned by Kent; and is painted with the ſtory of Hellenore and Malbecco*, by Scleter. It is adorned, in the front, with the buſts of Nero, Veſpaſian, Cleopatra, and Fauſtina. Over the freeze is the following motto alluding to the painting, from a Poem aſcribed to Catullus.

> Nunc amet, qui nunquam amavit;
> Quique amavit, nunc amet.

Thus tranſlated by Parnell.

> Let him love now, who never lov'd before;
> Let him who ever lov'd, now love the more.

The BELVIDERE, or Gibbes's Building. Underneath is an Ice-Houſe.

The ROMAN BOXERS, admirably copied.

* Spencer's Fairy Queen, B. III, C. 3.

TWO PAVILIONS. One of them is used as a Dwelling House; the other is ornamented with the Statues of Julius Cæsar, Cicero, Portia, and Livia.

The ÆGYPTIAN PYRAMID, which is 60 feet in height, with this Inscription. "Inter plurima hortorum horum ædificia a Johanne Vanbrugh, equite, designata, hanc Pyramidem illius memoriæ sacram voluit Cobham."

That is, "*Among the many edifices in these gardens designed by Sir John Vanbrugh, Cobham dedicates this in particular, to His Memory.*"

Within is the following Inscription from Horace.

"Lusisti satis, edisti satis, atque bibisti,
"Tempus abire tibi est; ne potum largis æquo
"Rideat et pulset lasciva decentius ætas."

Thus translated on the spot.
"Enough, my friend, you've trifled, drank and eat,
"'Tis time, at least 'tis prudence to retreat;
"Lest wanton Boys exert their decent rage,
"And kick you drunk and reeling from the stage."

The STATUES of HERCULES and ANTÆUS, situated in a FIELD, enclosed with a fence of stakes, after the military manner.

St. AUGUSTINE's CAVE, a monastic cell, built with moss and roots: Within is a straw couch, and several Latin Inscriptions, which are extremely happy in the stile of the old monkish Latin verse, and said to have been composed by Mr. Glover, the ingenious author of *Leonidas*.

The TEMPLE of BACCHUS, an edifice of brick: It's inside is adorned with Bacchanalian Scenes, painted by Nollikins. Among the rest, are two Vases in a masterly taste. Some of the smaller figures, in particular, are worth our attention.

A small

A small OBELISK, with this Inscription, "To the Memory of ROBIN COUCHER."

The SAXON TEMPLE. An altar situated in an open grove.

NELSON's SEAT. This is an elegant little building, from whence there is an agreeable open prospect: In the inside are Inscriptions, explaining the Paintings, in which the Boys fixing the Trophies are elegantly fancied.

The Equestrian STATUE of King GEORGE the First in armour, placed at the Head of the Canal, opposite the North Front of the House, with this Inscription from Virgil:

In medio mihi Cæsar erit——
Et viridi in Campo Signum de Marmore ponam
Propter Aquam.   COBHAM.

Thus translated:
"Full in the midst shall Cæsar's form divine
"Auspicious stand, the Godhead of the Shrine.—
"And near the stream a Marble Statue rear."

The STATUE of His late MAJESTY, raised on a Corinthian Pillar, with this Inscription:

Georgio Augusto.
That is, "To George Augustus."

DIDO's CAVE; a retired dark Building, with this Inscription, from Virgil:

Speluncam Dido, dux et Trojanus, eandem
Deveniunt.——

Thus translated on the spot:
"To the safe covert of one Cavern came
"The Trojan Leader, and the Tyrian Dame."

The ROTUNDA, supported by Ionic Pillars, and designed by Sir John Vanbrugh. Within, is a Statue of Venus de Medicis on a Pedestal of blue Marble.— Scarce any Object in the whole Garden shews itself more advantage, or makes a more beautiful figure, from several different points of prospect.

The STATUE of the late QUEEN, erected on four Ionic Columns, and situated in a rural Amphitheatre; with this Inscription:

Honori, Laudi, Virtuti, Divæ Carolinæ.

That is, "To the Honour, Praise, and Virtue of the divine Caroline."

The SLEEPING PARLOUR; a square building with an elegant Ionic Portico, situated in a close wood, with this Inscription:

Cum omnia sint in incerto, fave tibi.

That is, "Since all things are uncertain, take your pleasure."

The WITCH HOUSE; a square building. The Paintings on the walls are done by the late Lord's Gentleman; and though rude and inartificial, are much in character.

The TEMPLE of MODERN VIRTUE; *in Ruins*.

The TEMPLE of ANCIENT VIRTUE; a complete and beautiful Rotunda of the Ionic Order, designed by Kent. Over each door, on the outside, is this Motto: "PRISCÆ VIRTUTI." That is, *To ancient Virtue*. In four niches within, standing at full length, are the following Statues:

EPAMINONDAS, } { SOCRATES,
LYCURGUS,   } { HOMER.

Next are APOLLO and the NINE MUSES.

The SHELL-BRIDGE leads us over the Serpentine River into the *Elysian* Fields; and here we cannot omit giving the following Lines, which were left by a Gentleman unknown on his entering them.

To Lord COBHAM.

Charm'd with the Sight, my ravish'd Breast is fir'd
With Hints like those which ancient Bards inspir'd;
All

All the feign'd Tales by Superstition told,
All the bright Train of fabled Nymphs of Old,
Th' enthusiastic Muse believes, are true;
Thinks the spot sacred, and it's Genius You.
Lost in wild Rapture, would she fain disclose,
How by Degrees the pleasing wonder rose;
Industrious in a faithful Verse to trace
The various Beauties of the lovely Place;
And, while she keeps the glowing Work in View,
Thro' every Maze your artful Hand pursue.——

The TEMPLE of BRITISH WORTHIES.

In the Niches are the following Busto's.

POPE. Without an Inscription.

The person who left the following Lines on this great Poet's Busto best knows what he meant by them.

For LOVE some worship, some for FEAR:
Ask'st thou my Friend how POPE came here?

Sir THOMAS GRESHAM, who by the honourable Profession of a Merchant, having enriched himself and Country, for carrying on the Commerce of the World, built the *Royal Exchange.*

IGNATIUS JONES, who, to adorn his Country, introduced and rivaled the *Greek* and *Roman* Architecture.

JOHN MILTON, whose sublime and unbounded Genius equalled a Subject that carried him beyond the Limits of the World.

WILLIAM SHAKESPEAR, whose excellent Genius opened to him the whole Heart of Man, all the Mines of Fancy, all the Stores of Nature; and gave him Powers beyond all other Writers, to move, astonish, and delight Mankind.

JOHN LOCKE, who, best of all Philosophers, understood the Powers of the Human Mind, the Nature, End, and Bounds of Civil Government; and with equal Courage and Sagacity, refuted the slavish Systems of
usurped

usurped Authority over the Rights, the Consciences, or the Reason of Mankind.

Sir ISAAC NEWTON, whom the God of Nature made to comprehend his Works; and from simple Principles, to discover the Laws never known before, and to explain the Appearance never understood, of this stupendous Universe.

Sir FRANCIS BACON, Lord *Verulam*, who, by the Strength and Light of a superior Genius, rejecting vain Speculation, and fallacious Theory, taught to pursue Truth, and improve Philosophy by the certain Method of Experiment.

In the Nich of a Pyramid is placed a Mercury, with these Words subscribed:

—— *Campos ducit ad Elysios.*

That is, "Leads to the *Elysian* Fields."

And below this Figure is fixed a square black Marble, with the following Lines:

Hic manus ob patriam pugnando vulnera passi,
Quique pii vates, & Phœbo digna locuti,
Inventas aut qui vitam excoluere per artes,
Quique sui memores alios fecere merendo.

Here are the Bards who for their Country bled,
And Bards whose pure and sacred Verse is read:
Those who, by Arts invented, Life improv'd;
And by their Merits made their Mem'ries lov'd.

KING ALFRED, the mildest, justest, most beneficent of Kings; who drove out the *Danes*, secured the Seas, protected Learning, established Justice, crushed Corruption, guarded Liberty, and was the Founder of the *English* Constitution.

EDWARD Prince of *Wales*, the Terror of *Europe*, the Delight of *England*; who preserved, unaltered in the Height of Glory and Fortune, his natural Gentleness and Modesty.

QUEEN ELIZABETH, who confounded the Projects

jects and destroyed the Power that threatened to oppress the Liberties of *Europe*; took off the Yoke of Ecclesiastical Tyranny; restored Religion from the Corruption of *Popery*; and by a wise, a moderate, and a popular Government, gave Wealth, Security, and Respect to *England*.

KING WILLIAM III. who, by his Virtue and Constancy, having saved his Country, from a foreign Master, by a bold and generous Enterprize, preserved the Liberty and Religion of *Great Britain*.

Sir WALTER RALEIGH, a valiant Soldier, and an able Statesman; who endeavouring to rouse the Spirit of his Master, for the Honour of his Country, against the Ambition of *Spain*, fell a Sacrifice to the Influence of that Court, whose Arms he had vanquished, and whose Designs he opposed.

Sir FRANCIS DRAKE, who, through many Perils, was the first of *Britons* that adventured to sail round the Globe; and carried into unknown Seas and Nations the Knowlege and Glory of the *English* Name.

JOHN HAMPDEN, who with great Spirit and consummate Abilities, begun a noble Opposition to an arbitrary Court, in Defence of the Liberties of his Country; supported them in Parliament, and died for them in the Field.

Sir JOHN BARNARD, without any Inscription.

Behind this Building is a Monument with this Inscription:

To the Memory of
SIGNIOR FIDO,
An *Italian* of good Extraction;
Who came into *England*,
Not to bite us, like most of his Countrymen,
But to gain an honest Livelihood;
He hunted not after Fame,
Yet acquired it;
Regardless of the Praise of his Friends,

But

But most sensible of their Love.
Tho' he lived amongst the Great,
He neither learnt nor flatter'd any Vice.
He was no Bigot,
Tho' he doubted of none of the XXXIX Articles.
And, if to follow Nature
And respect the Laws of Society,
Be Philosophy,
He was a perfect Philosopher;
A faithful Friend,
An agreeable Companion,
A loving Husband,
Distinguish'd by a numerous Offspring,
All which he lived to see take good Courses.
In his old Age he retir'd
To the House of a Clergyman in the Country,
Where he finished his earthly Race,
And died an Honour and an Example to the whole
Species.
READER,
This Stone is guiltless of Flattery,
For he to whom it is inscribed
Was not a Man,
But a
GREY-HOUND.

The SHELL-BRIDGE.

The CHINESE HOUSE stands on a large Piece of Water. The Outside is painted by Mr. *Sleter*, after the *Chinese* Manner. Within is a *Chinese* Figure of a Lady asleep.

The TEMPLE of CONTEMPLATION.

The GROTTO at the Head of the Serpentine River, is furnished with a Number of Looking-Glasses, both on the Walls and Cieling, in Frames of Plaister-Work, stuck with Shells and Flint. In it is a Marble Statue of *Venus*.

The LADIES TEMPLE, supported by Arches, with *Venetian* Windows. On one Side is a Painting of Ladies employing themselves at Needle and Shell Work; on the other, Ladies at Music and Painting, both by *Sleter*.

The GRECIAN TEMPLE is a large Building of the *Ionic* Order, said to be in Imitation of the Temple of *Minerva* at *Athens*.

Captain GRENVILLE's Monument, on which is the following Inscription:

Sororis suæ Filio,
THOMÆ GRENVILLE,
Qui navis Præfectus regiæ,
Ducente classem Britannicam Georgio Anson
Dum contra Gallos fortissimè pugnaret,
Dilaceratæ navis ingenti fragmine
Femore graviter percusso,
Perire, dixit moribundus, omnino satius esse,
Quam inertiæ reum in judicio sisti;
Columnam hanc rostratam
Laudans & mærens posuit
COBHAM.
Insigne virtutis, eheu! rarissimæ
Exemplum habes;
Ex quo discas
Quid virum præfectura militari ornatum
Deceat.
M. DCC. XLVII.

As a Monument
To testify his Applause and Grief,
RICHARD Lord Viscount COBHAM
Erected this Naval Pillar to the Memory of his Nephew
CAPTAIN GRENVILLE;
Who, commanding a Ship of War in the *British* Fleet
Under ADMIRAL ANSON,
In an Engagement with the *French*,

Was

Was mortally wounded in the Thigh
By a Fragment of his shatter'd Ship.
Dying, he cried out,
"How much more defirable is it thus to meet Death,
"Than, fufpected of Cowardice, to fear Juftice!"
May this noble Inftance of Virtue
Prove inftructive to an abandoned Age,
And teach *Britons* how to act
In their Country's Caufe?

A Spacious BASON of WATER, defigned for the Triumphal Arch.

A FLUTED COLUMN, erected to the Memory of the late Lord COBHAM.

On one Side.
To preferve the Memory of her Hufband,
ANNE, Vicountefs COBHAM,
Caufed this Pillar to be erected
In the Year 1747.

On the oppofite Side.
Quatenus nobis denegatur diu vivere,
relinquamus aliquid,
quo nos vixiffe teftemur.

As we cannot live long,
Let us leave fomething behind us,
to fhew we have lived.

The GOTHIC TEMPLE, with this Infcription:
Je rends graces aux dieux de n'eftre pas Romain.
That is, "I return Thanks to the Gods for not be-
"ing a *Roman.*

The Infide of the Dome is decorated with the Arms of his Lordfhip's Family, from their Rife to the prefent Time.

The PALLADIAN BRIDGE, on which are feveral Antique Marble Bufto's. It is fupported by *Ionic* Pillars on the Side facing the Water. The Black-Wall is adorned with a Piece of Alto-Relievo, by Mr. *Schee-maker,*

maker, representing the Four Quarters of the World bringing their various Products to *Britannia*.

The IMPERIAL CLOSET is a square Room, in which are painted in Fresco by *Sclet*— the three Humane *Roman* Emperors, each of wh— —distinguished by a memorable saying of his own.

IMP. TITUS CÆS. VESPASI—
Diem perdidi.———
I have lost a Day.

IMP. N. TRAJAN CÆS. AU.
Pro me: si merear, in me.
For me:———if I deserve it, against me.

IMP. MARCUS AURELIUS CÆSAR ANTONINUS.
Ita regnes imperator, ut privatus, regi te velis.
So govern if a King, as you would be governed if a Subject.

The Grand TERRAS-WALK, 300 Feet long, where is a STATUE of a GLADIATOR, brings us to

The TEMPLE of FRIENDSHIP. A Structure of the *Doric* Order, with this Motto on the Outside,
Amicitiæ S. Sacred to Friendship.
On the Roof are emblematical Paintings alluding to Friendship and Liberty. *Britannia* is represented sitting in State with Labels on one Side inscribed *Edward* III. and Queen *Elizabeth*; on the other she is presented with the Reign of ———, which she covers with her Mantle, unwilling to look at it. The Inside is furnished with the Busts of the late Lord and his illustrious Friends, *viz. Frederick* Prince of *Wales*, the Earls of *Chesterfield, Westmorland*, and *Marchmont*; the Lords *Cobham, Gower*, and *Bathurst*; the present Earl, Lord *Littleton*, and *William Pitt*, Esq;

The PEBBLE ALCOVE is a little Grot, on which are his Lordship's Arms on the Back Wall.

CONGREVE's MONUMENT, with Embellishments designed to express the Poet's Comic Genius.

On the Top is a Monkey viewing himself in a Mirror, with the following Inscription:

Vitæ imitatio,
Consuetudinis speculum,
Comœdia.

Comedy, Imitation of Life, and the Mirror of Fashion.

The Effigy of the Poet lies in a careless Posture, with this Epitaph:

Ingenio
Acri, faceto, expolito,
Moribusque
Urbanis, candidis, facilimis,
GULIELMI CONGREVE,
Hoc
Qualecunque desiderii sui
Solamen simul &
Monumentum,
Posuit COBHAM.
1736.

That is, "To the piercing, facetious, and refined "Wit, to the polished, candid, and unaffected Man- "ners of WILLIAM CONGREVE, hath COBHAM erected "this poor Consolation for, the Monument of, his "Loss. 1736."

FINIS.

New-College Chapel.

AS the Painted Windows of this Chapel make one of it's chief Ornaments, it will not be improper to bestow on them a more particular Description.

Of those there are four distinct Sorts.

1. All the windows of the Ante Chapel (the great one excepted) are nearly, if not quite, as old as the Chapel itself, and contain the pourtraits of Patriarchs, Prophets, Saints, Martyrs, &c. to the number of 64, and 50 smaller above them: Curious for their antiquity, but for little else, being drawn without perspective, without the effect of light and shade, and ill-proportioned; yet in these are some remains which shew the brilliancy of their colours, and some traces of simplicity and beauty; particularly in the heads of the female figures in the

the window on the right hand of the entrance to the Chapel.

2. Of the second sort are the Windows on the North side of the Chapel. These are done in the common modern stile by Mr. *Peckitt* of *York*. The three nearest the Organ contain, in the lower range, the chief persons recorded in the Old Testament from *Adam* to *Moses*; in the upper, twelve of the Prophets. Mr. *Rebecca* gave the designs for these. The two other windows (when completed) will contain our Saviour, the Virgin Mary, and the twelve Apostles.

3. The third sort are on the South side of the Chapel. These were originally *Flemish* windows; and done (as it is reported) from designs given by some scholars of *Rubens*. Being brought out of *Flanders*, they came into the possession of *Price* the son, whose skill in Glasspainting is well known. Of him they were purchased by

by the Gentlemen of the College, who also employed him to repair what injuries they had sustained, and to fit them for the places where they now stand *A. D.* 1740. In each window are eight figures of Saints, Martyrs and Prelates with their respective symbols; and for expression, colouring, and effect, they were esteemed equal, if not superior, to any painting executed on Glass till the appearance of the fourth sort, of which we now come to speak.

4. The West window of the Ante Chapel. This great window consists of seven compartments in the lower range, each near three feet wide and twelve high. In these stand seven allegorical figures, representing the four Cardinal, and three Christian Virtues, in the manner following:

TEMPERANCE, pouring water out of a larger vessel into a small one. Her common attribute, the Bridle, lies as her feet.

(4)

FORTITUDE, in armour; her hand resting on a broken column, which though half destroyed remains upright; her form robust, her look bold and resolute. A Lion, her attendant, couches below her.

FAITH, standing fixedly on both feet, and bearing a Cross, the symbol of her belief; her eyes and hand raised up to Heaven.

On the other side of the middle group (of which more hereafter) HOPE, looking toward the same Heaven, and springing forward to it so eagerly that her feet scarce touch the ground. Part of an Anchor, her attribute, is seen in the corner of her compartment.

JUSTICE, looking with a steady and piercing eye through the dark shade which her arm casts over her face: in her left hand the Steelyard; a kind of balance less cumbrous, if not less vulgar, than the scales which are usually given her. Her right hand supports the sword.

PRUDENCE,

PRUDENCE, beholding (as in a mirror) the actions and manners of others, for the purpose of regulating her own by obfervation thereon. Upon her right arm an Arrow joined with a Remora, the refpective emblems of fwiftnefs and flownefs; Prudence being a medium between them.

The middle groupe, mentioned above, reprefents CHARITY, and deferves efpecial notice for the expreffion of the figures therein contained. The fondling of the Infant, the importunity of the Boy, and the placid affection of the Girl, together with the divided attention of the Mother, are all diftinguifhably and judicioufly marked with a knowledge of character for which the great Artift who gave this defign is fo juftly celebrated.

Such are the figures which fill the lower compartments; yet they are but a fubordinate part, and (as it were) a bafis to the fuperb work erected over them. In a fpace ten feet wide

wide and eighteen high is reprefented the NATIVITY of JESUS CHRIST: a compofition of thirteen human figures befide other animals. 1. The bleffed Virgin, whofe attention is wholly engaged in her Infant. 2. A groupe of Angels defcended into the ftable, and kneeling around him. The face of the leaft of thefe exhibits an idea of youthful beauty that perhaps was never furpaffed. 3. A company of Shepherds, whofe devotion and rude eagernefs to behold him are ftrongly expreffed. 4. St. *Jofeph*, looking on the fpectators, and pointing to the Child, as *to the promifed feed, the expectation and hope of all Nations*. 5. In the clouds above, an Angel contemplating the myftery of the Crofs; and near him a Scroll, whereon is written the original Greek of this text, *Myfteries which the Angels themfelves defire to look into*.

In this compofition the Painter has taken for his light that which is fuppofed posed to proceed from the body of the Infant: herein imitating a famous picture now preserved in the Gallery at *Dresden*, and known by the name of the *Notte of Corregio*.* This beautiful idea has often been adopted, but never so judiciously applied as in this instance; where the substance on which the Infant is delineated being transparent, and the light actually passing through him, his body thereby receives a higher glow, and gives to the whole an appearance of reality.

The remaining parts of this grand design (not yet completed) are to consist of groups of Shepherds and other persons who are approaching the Stable to pay their devotions to the new-born Saviour.

For this work, which was begun about seven years ago, finished Cartoons were furnished by Sir *Joshua*

* A small copy of this picture is in the Collection at Christ Church.

Reynolds.

Reynolds. These were copied by Mr. *Jervais*; to whose skill the world is indebted for a new stile in Glass-painting, which in beauty and truth of representation exceeds all that have hitherto been seen, as much as the common productions excel the first rude attempts of the art.

www.ingramcontent.com/pod-product-compliance
Lightning Source LLC
Chambersburg PA
CBHW020255170426
43202CB00008B/386